SPEECH
FROM
THE DOCK

by
Bishop
DONAL LAMONT

KEVIN MAYHEW
Publishers

in association with
CATHOLIC INSTITUTE
for
INTERNATIONAL RELATIONS

First published in Great Britain in 1977 by
KEVIN MAYHEW LTD
55 Leigh Road
Leigh-on-Sea, Essex

in association with
CATHOLIC INSTITUTE
for
INTERNATIONAL RELATIONS
1 Cambridge Terrace
Regent's Park
London NW1 4JL

ISBN 0 905725 29 8

Printed and bound by E T Heron & Co Ltd, Essex
and London

CONTENTS

INTRODUCTION

On Wednesday 23rd March 1977 Donal Lamont, the sixty-five year old Bishop of Umtali, was stripped of his Rhodesian citizenship and deported. This deportation marked the end of more than thirty years of ministry in Rhodesia and was the culmination of the régime's attempts to silence a consistently critical voice. Bishop Lamont had over the years become the symbol of the Church's conflict with the state on the rights of African Rhodesians to self-determination.

Bishop Lamont's deportation came at the end of an appeal against a ten-year prison sentence with labour, imposed on him by the Rhodesian courts in October 1976. He had pleaded guilty to four counts of failing to report the presence of guerrillas and of telling others to do likewise. The imposition of this sentence provoked a storm of international protest. Telegrams of support from religious and political leaders throughout the world flooded into Rhodesia; among them were messages from Pope Paul and Jimmy Carter.

While the international community wholeheartedly commended his identification with the aspirations of the black Rhodesian majority, Bishop Lamont was regarded by the Rhodesian government as a menace and by most white Rhodesians as a traitor.

To understand the predicament of Christian missionaries in present-day Rhodesia, we must remember the nature of the society in which they exercise their ministry. Rhodesia is a country of over six million blacks and two hundred and fifty thousand whites. White Rhodesians have total political control of the country and are the beneficiaries of a grossly inegalitarian economic system. They occupy over half the land and have access to the most productive land in the country. In spite of United Nations sanctions living standards for white Rhodesians have risen considerably in the last twelve years and compare favourably with all western countries. In contrast, the vast majority of black Rhodesians live in poverty and are excluded from political life. Over the past ten years the differential between black and white average earnings has doubled. A senior welfare officer has recently estimated that some seventy-five per cent of urban Africans in Bulawayo where the breadwinner is in employment have incomes below subsistence levels, and this pattern is repeated throughout the country. All attempts to change this situation through constitutional means have failed.

Rhodesia is in practice a police state: strikes are effectively banned, the media are controlled, many political organisations are prohibited, whole communities are uprooted and forced to live as virtual prisoners in the so-called protected villages. Laws have been enacted giving the Security Forces a blank cheque for any atrocities they wish to commit. Hundreds of people have been tried and executed in secret. Torture, intimidation and killings by the Security Forces are the order of the day.

Over the last few years the white minority has had to pay an ever-increasing price for the privileges it enjoys. The escalating civil war has affected virtually every Rhodesian home. Call-up into the armed forces has been progressively tightened. All white, coloured and asian males must, on leaving school, register with the armed forces and from that time, if they are under thirty, are not allowed to leave the country without special permission. After serving an initial eighteen months they are liable to be called up every few months. This total mobilisation of the white community puts immense strain on family life and, of course, on the Rhodesian economy.

The resulting low morale and confusion among whites has been intensified by the Rhodesia Front's apparent concession to the principle of majority rule. Many whites wonder exactly what they are fighting for. The loss of morale is reflected in emigration figures. During 1976 immigration statistics showed a net loss of some seven thousand people. This figure does not accurately reflect the true extent of emigration. The recruitment of between 1,200 and 1,600 mercenaries distorts this figure. Emigration would be massive but for the difficulty of selling assets and the stringent exchange control regulations. Indeed many people emigrate under the guise of taking a holiday because for a variety of reasons they do not want the government to know they are leaving the country. This hidden emigration does not, of course, appear in statistics.

If the war has seriously disrupted white Rhodesian society, its impact on African life has been disastrous. Hundreds of thousands of people have been forcibly driven from their homes and packed into 'protected villages' where in general conditions are appalling. Government propaganda portrays the 'protected villages' as being for the Africans' own protection, designed to be centres of development and a way of shortening the war against Communism by starving the guerrillas of their food supply. In fact most 'protected villages' are centres of hardship and misery – there is serious overcrowding, sanitary conditions are rudimentary and medical and welfare facilities are inadequate. The villagers are unable to tend their cattle and their lands properly and their crops, if they are not destroyed by the Security Forces, may be ruined by animals. A strict curfew is in operation in many areas which poses particular problems for rural Africans whose land is some distance from the 'protected village'. Curfew breakers are often shot without warning. Mr Ian Smith admitted that up to 24th February 1977, 632 Africans had been killed and 294 wounded 'while breaking the curfew or running with and assisting terrorists'.

CHURCH AND STATE IN RHODESIA

Some cynics have accused the Church in Rhodesia of jumping on the bandwagon of African nationalism. However, the stand taken by the Church is not a recent one. Bishop Lamont's pastoral letter, *Purchased People,* issued in 1959, marked the beginning of the tension between Church and state in Rhodesia. The pastoral letter was by no means radical but it was the first time that a Bishop in Rhodesia had drawn such attention to the injustices of Rhodesian society and had identified himself with African aspirations:

If nationalism as it manifests itself here among the African people means the desire of that people to participate fully in the life and in the development of their country; if it means a will to hold on to the things which they believe to have a traditional and cultural value and which are not contrary to the Moral Law; if it means a refusal to be stripped of their ancient character and turned out in mass-production, de-characterised and presented to the world as ersatz Europeans; or if it means a sincere and simple wish to be regarded by all and to be treated by the State as equal citizens, and not as second-class citizens, then obviously such aspirations are beyond reproach and the Church must support them.

The other Bishops refused to sign the pastoral letter and it was not until two years later that they issued their first joint pastoral letter, *Peace Through Justice*. In it they denounced racial discrimination and argued that 'there can be no stability in society while the few possess much and the majority have little or nothing'. They insisted that racial harmony 'is not simply one of social adjustment but of social justice. It is essentially a moral problem, a problem of right and wrong. When fundamental human rights are denied to any people, simply because of their race, a grievous wrong is perpetrated.'

Since that time at least thirteen joint statements have been made by the Rhodesian Catholic Bishops' Conference and also a number of statements by Bishop Lamont, which trace the increasing hostility in Church-State relations and the growing determination of the Church to speak out against injustice.

In 1965 Mr Ian Smith made his Unilateral Declaration of Independence and said in an address to the nation: 'We have struck a blow for the preservation of justice, civilisation and Christianity, and in the spirit of this belief we have this day assumed our sovereign independence'. Shortly afterwards the Bishops issued an outspoken and critical pastoral letter, *A Plea for Peace*.

The government censorship office in Salisbury censored the Shona and Ndebele translations of the letter and the Bishops subsequently refused to publish this censored version. One of the deleted passages read:

Another thing which is quite clear to us is this: vast numbers of the people of Rhodesia are bitterly opposed to the Unilateral Declaration of Independence made recently. They are particularly angered that it should be stated publicly that this action was taken in the name of preserving Christian civilisation in this country. It is simply quite untrue to say that the masses are content with this recent decision or that they have consented by their silence. Their silence is the silence of fear, of disappointment, of hopelessness. It is dangerous silence; dangerous for the Church, for all of us.

It comes as no surprise, therefore, that many are saying: 'So this is Christian civilisation! This is what Christianity is! The preservation of privilege for the few and well-to-do, and the neglect of the many who have nothing!' They also say: 'It seems as if we have been deceived by the exponents of Christianity, the missionaries. These have come here only to prepare the way for the racist state where we shall remain permanently the hewers of wood and drawers of water, and where a favoured handful can control and delay our development indefinitely.'

The Bishops were equally outspoken in their criticisms of the 1969 Constitution in their pastoral letter *A Call to Christians,* published in June that year. The 1969 Constitution was much more racist than the mildly liberal 1961 Constitution. In their letter the Bishops said:

the proposals for the new Constitution are in many ways completely contrary to Christian teaching and we must therefore reject them for the benefit of our own people and on behalf of all men of good will publicly condemn them.

Indeed the Bishops have taken care to maintain throughout this conflict that their obligation to speak has been based on moral rather than political criteria; their primary concern has been for human rights. They have been criticised for their lack of political ideology and their failure to suggest concrete action to black Rhodesians faced with urgent political decisions.

Whilst these pastoral letters were signed by all the Bishops, their style and tone is that of Bishop Lamont. It is interesting to contrast the tone of earlier pastoral letters with Bishop Lamont's *Open Letter to the Rhodesian Government* issued on 11th August 1976. This Open Letter was written as Umtali was being shelled from Mozambique in retaliation for the Rhodesian army's massacre of hundreds of men, women and children in a refugee/training camp in Mozambique. It was probably this letter which finally provoked the Rhodesian régime into taking action to silence him, although the régime has publicly denied this. In it Bishop Lamont says:

Conscience compels me to state that your administration by its clearly racist and oppressive policies and by its stubborn refusal to change, is largely responsible for the injustices which have provoked the present disorder and it must in that measure be considered guilty of whatever misery or bloodshed may follow.

Far from your policies defending Christianity and Western Civilisation, as you claim, they mock the law of Christ and make Communism attractive to the African people . . . On whatever dubious grounds you may at one time have based your claim to rule, such argument no longer has any validity. You may rule with the consent of a small and selfish electorate, but you rule without the consent of the nation, which is the test of all legitimacy.

Many people, particularly inside Rhodesia, regard Bishop Lamont as a left-wing revolutionary, a sort of Rhodesian Camillo Torres. He is not. His theological formation is firmly rooted in mainstream Catholic-orthodox thought and is not derived from Latin American liberation theology or radical European political theology.

THE WAR

After a period of sporadic incursions beginning in late 1964, nationalist guerrillas launched a sustained offensive in north-east Rhodesia in December 1972. Since then, in the period up to March 1977, over 4,000 people have been killed – more than 2,727 guerrillas, more than 256 soldiers including a number of South African Police and some 1,473 civilians, including 79 whites. The figure for civilian dead include some 632 who the government admit have been killed by the Security Forces for breaking the curfew or 'running with' the guerrillas. These are official government figures and therefore need to be treated with caution. They do, however, give some indication of the nature and the scale of the war.

Since 1972 the war has escalated not only in terms of numbers of people involved in the fighting, but also in terms of the areas in which the fighting is taking place. Since the collapse of the Portuguese Empire, the major guerrilla offensive has been from across the Mozambique border. However, guerrillas are operating from each of the countries bordering Rhodesia, with the exception of South Africa. There are now very few rural areas in Rhodesia where there is no guerrilla presence and reliable sources indicate that guerrillas are establishing themselves in the urban townships. According to government estimates there are currently some 2,500 guerrillas operating inside the country. This figure does not include the countless numbers of Rhodesians who give material and other support to the guerrillas. The insurgents are able to melt in with the local population. They travel in small groups and rely on the local people for information, food and shelter.

The Rhodesian Security Forces are well aware that no guerrillas could operate inside the country without at least the tacit consent of the local people. They have, therefore, adopted policies of systematic harassment, intimidation and torture both to extract information about guerrilla movements and to deter potential supporters of the liberation struggle. One of the most controversial issues in the counter-insurgency campaign is the use of the Selous Scouts, a commando unit operating throughout the country. They often masquerade as guerrillas and exact retribution from those Africans who co-operate with them in this guise. By committing atrocities in the guise of guerrillas they aim to confuse and alienate the local people and to test their loyalty. The resulting dilemma was well expressed by one old villager who said: "If we report the terrorists, they destroy our homes and fields and come and kill us. If we do not report them the soldiers come to torture us and to destroy our homes and fields. But even if we report the terrorists, the soldiers torture us all the same, for they think we are just trying to set them up."

The civil war in Rhodesia presents missionaries with difficult moral choices. Missionaries, although often white and albeit expatriate, live and work in mainly rural areas. They are thus an integral part of the local community. They are involved not only with the spiritual welfare of their parishioners but with the life of the community at all levels. Missionaries in rural areas make an essential contribution to health, education and community development. The problems and concerns of the community are therefore shared by missionaries.

When the Security Forces move into an area, uproot the local people and move them into 'protected villages', bomb their houses and destroy their crops, harass and torture people on suspicion of harbouring terrorists, shoot civilians on their way home from having a beer or tending their cattle, the missionaries cannot help but be involved. It is their own communities which are in danger. The people come to them for help and advice in the face of the Rhodesian government's policies. The missionaries experience with them the injustice of the system and share with them the desire for change. It is therefore not surprising that so many missionaries identify with the aspirations of their parishioners for a new and more just society.

Nor is it a situation in which the missionary can remain neutral. The régime defines the guerrillas as 'communist terrorists' and demands total loyalty from the missionary in its efforts to wipe them out – even that he should act as informer on the movements of the insurgents. Not to inform the authorities when this occurs is a criminal offence. At the same time the missionary knows that if he notifies the authorities, the army is likely to saturate the area and exact terrible and indiscriminate retribution from the local people for assisting the guerrillas. What is the missionary to do?

Even those who do not feel that the guerrilla war is justified are convinced that the repressive policies of the régime have provoked the war. If it can be argued that the guerrillas have no legitimacy, it can be argued with greater force that neither does the present Rhodesian government. Is the execution of informants by the guerrillas any more illegal than the judicial murder of civilians by the illegal régime? The régime accuses the guerrillas of irresponsibility but has itself sanctioned irresponsibility on the part of the Security Forces by the enactment of laws such as the Indemnity and Compensation Act.

This still leaves the question of whether armed struggle is morally justifiable. Contrary to western myth, the conscience of the guerrillas has been formed not by Marxist indoctrination but largely by Christian teaching in the mission schools. The Catholic Bishops have proposed the conditions for armed revolt in their first joint pastoral letter:

It must never be forgotten that only an insupportable tyranny or flagrant violation of the most obvious essential rights of the citizens, can give, after every other means of redress have failed, the right to revolt against the legitimate authority.

The decision whether or not to resort to violence as a means of overthrowing tyranny is a difficult one and

15

can only be taken by those who are actually involved in the situation. It is clear that the vast majority of black Rhodesians have decided that the present Rhodesian régime is tyrannical and without legitimacy. They believe that all attempts to achieve their rights by peaceful means have failed. The guerrilla war is thus seen by them as an essential element in the overthrow of the régime.

THE LAMONT CASE

As the war intensified, increasing numbers of Africans mainly from rural areas made their way to the Justice and Peace Commission office in Salisbury with complaints of their treatment at the hands of the Security Forces. As the demands became more pressing, the Commission felt compelled to investigate the allegations and to take up the matter with the Rhodesian government.

The role of Bishop Lamont in the Commission, which was formed in 1972 and is an official body of the Roman Catholic hierarchy, was certainly a contributory factor to his deportation. The Rhodesian Commission has focused much of its attention on investigating allegations of brutality and murder of Africans by members of the Rhodesian Security Forces. Such investigations have inevitably attracted hostility from the Rhodesia Front government and its supporters. The officers of the régime – Security Forces, police, chiefs and any public servants – are protected from criticism by a series of 'emergency laws'. In publishing reports of carefully investigated cases of torture, intimidation and killings of Africans by Security Forces, in particular *The Man in the Middle* (May 1975) and *Civil War in Rhodesia* (October 1976) the Commission has taken up the gauntlet, strongly challenging the actions of the régime and its officers.

The government has accused the Commission of being a 'fifth column' and has used every means at its disposal to discredit its work. In September 1976 the Commission's president, Bishop Lamont, was charged. His trial symbolised the missionaries' dilemma and indeed almost any other missionary could have found himself in the dock faced with similar charges.

Aware of the significance of his trial, Bishop Lamont made a lengthy unsworn statement to the court. On the advice of his counsel, he did not make his statement on oath – not because he was afraid of cross-examination but for three very good reasons. First he wanted to avoid having nuns called as witnesses against their bishop. Secondly he wanted the freedom to make a general statement about the situation in Rhodesia and not be confined to the technicalities of the charges levelled against him. Thirdly he thought an oath unnecessary since he was pleading guilty. The full text of his oral statement is printed in full and is the main part of this book.

The Appeal Court judgement in Bishop Lamont's case is a masterpiece of legal indiscretion. Justice MacDonald introduces extraneous material not led in evidence and uses his position to give vent to his personal feelings on the role of the Church in society, the aims and objectives of the guerrilla movements and the development of Rhodesia as a country. The communist bogy looms large in the judgement. It assumed that black Rhodesians have no cause for dissatisfaction or for revolt against the Rhodesian government. It is his supremely paternalistic belief that white government has brought civilisation, stability and economic prosperity to Rhodesia.

17

According to him the guerrillas fight against the government because they are pawns of the communists. He condemns them as misguided, indoctrinated terrorists rather than freedom fighters who are attempting to overthrow a thoroughly corrupt and tyrannical régime. Justice MacDonald dismisses Bishop Lamont's indictment of the excesses of the Rhodesian Security Forces despite the overwhelming body of supportive evidence. He praises the achievements of the white régime, but glosses over the multiple and fundamental causes of the grievances which cause young African people to leave Rhodesia in droves to fight for the overthrow of the white minority government. The judgement is an apology for the white racist régime. He has no concept of the responsibilities of the Church in seeking social justice. He denies that the Church has an obligation in the sphere of temporal matters to oppose oppression, injustice and suffering and to refuse to comply with laws which have these effects.

CONCLUSION

It is hoped that this book will help to put into focus the stand taken by Bishop Lamont and many other missionaries in Rhodesia today. In Bishop Lamont's diocese alone, two priests, Fr Patrick Mutume and Fr Ignatius Mhonda, have been sentenced to four years' imprisonment (three years suspended) on similar charges and are waiting the decision of the Appeal Court. Both were assaulted in custody and Father Mhonda sustained a perforated ear-drum as a result of his treatment in detention. Both appeared at the local court handcuffed, barefooted and in prison garb. Fr Alexander Sakarombe was arrested and detained for eleven days. He has since been rearrested together with an Irish Carmelite priest, Fr Laurence Lynch.

It is hoped too that this book will provide a perspective for the tragic killings of missionaries which have taken place in Rhodesia recently. There are grave doubts as to who was responsible for their deaths and evidence is emerging which suggests that at least some of the murders were the work of the Selous Scouts. It is unlikely that the facts will ever be proven. However, if the massacre were perpetrated by guerrillas, it was a maverick band. It is certainly not the policy of the guerrilla movements. However, it would be naïve to believe that guerrilla groups do not commit atrocities against civilians and such actions are to be deplored and condemned. At the same time, whilst in no way excusing such deeds, they must be seen side by side with what is tantamount to a deliberate policy of systematic brutality on the part of the Security Forces. Accounts of intimidation, torture and killings of civilians by the Rhodesian Security Forces are numerous and well documented in the reports from the Rhodesian Catholic Justice and Peace Commission.

Indeed the Rhodesian government itself has acknowledged the substance of the many allegations contained in the reports by refusing an independent enquiry and by refusing the Commission's challenge to prosecute them for making false allegations – a crime in Rhodesia. Furthermore in 1975 the régime enacted the Indemnity and Compensation Act. This Act indemnifies from prosecution any public servant who commits *any act* 'in good faith' . . . 'for or in connexion with the suppression of terrorism'. This Act was made retrospective to 1st December 1972. As the Commission said in a statement of protest

19

about this Act, 'by thus exonerating the Security Forces in advance, this may amount to a mandate for illegalities'. This view was endorsed by the late Sir Robert Tredgold, the former Federal Chief Justice, who said: "It is contrary to the rule of law and to our own system to give protection in advance to acts of the Executive or its officials that are illegal or of questionable legality".

Tim Sheehy
Eileen Sudworth
C.I.I.R.
April 20, 1976

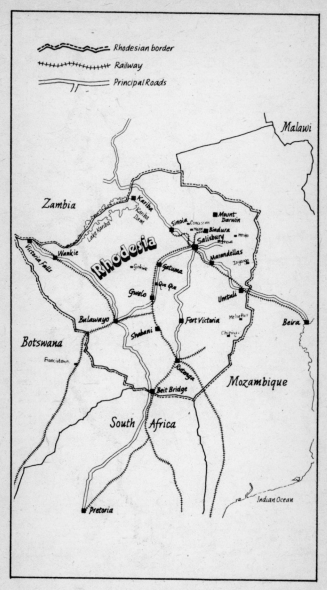

Rhodesian border
Railway
Principal Roads

Malawi

Zambia

Kariba
Kariba Dam
Lake Kariba
Sinoia · Concession · Mount Darwin
Msoe · Bindura
Salisbury
Arena
Victoria Falls
Wankie
Rhodesia
Gokwe · Gatuma
Marandellas
Inyanga
Gwelo
Que Que
Umtali
Bulawayo
Fort Victoria
Melsetter
Beira
Shabani
Chipinga
Botswana
Franciutown
Rusenga
Mozambique
Beit Bridge
South Africa
Indian Ocean
Pretoria

21

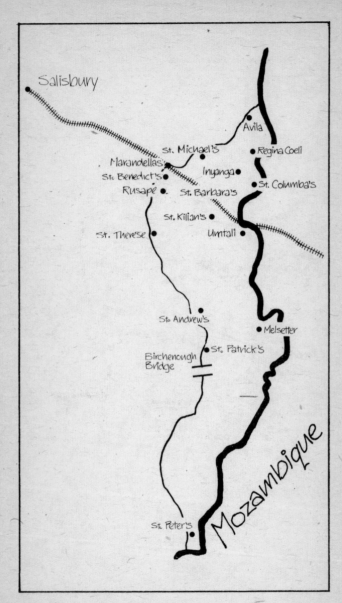

Salisbury

Avila

St. Michael's

Regina Coeli

Marandellas

Inyanga

St. Benedict's

St. Columba's

Rusape

St. Barbara's

St. Kilian's

St. Therese

Umtali

St. Andrew's

Melsetter

Birchenough
Bridge

St. Patrick's

Mozambique

St. Peter's

Speech from the Dock

MY PERSONAL HISTORY

I was born in 1911 in Northern Ireland into a middle class family of five boys and one girl. During my youth the Irish war of independence was being waged all around us. The establishment of the Irish Free State meant a turning point for the lives of many of us who supported the nationalist cause.

I completed my secondary education at Terenure College in Dublin, where I had moderate academic success but satisfactory results in everything connected with games. I mention this to show that I was a very normal kind of youth. I had represented my Province of Ulster in schools hockey. I also played for the first XV in rugby and was *Victor Ludorum* at the College sports.

Having finished school I felt called to the priesthood and joined the Carmelite Order. After a year spent as a novice I took vows of religion for three years, and during this time studied at University College, Dublin, where I read an honours course in English Language, Philology and English Literature. I gained an Honours Degree in 1933. My superiors then sent me to the international College of the Carmelites in Rome where I spent the next five years studying Philosophy and Theology. This Philosophy course included Logic, Metaphysics, Psychology, Ethics, Cosmology and the History of Philosophy. The course in Theology involved the study of Dogmatic and Moral Theology, Canon Law, Church History, Holy Scripture, including some knowledge of Hebrew and Greek, Patristics,

Ascetical and Pastoral Theology with the ancillary subjects, Christian Archaeology and Music. I had had some training in music and attended regularly as an external student the Pontifical Academy where I was particularly interested in Polyphony and Plain-song.

A most important feature of the years of study in Rome was that it brought me into contact with world opinion. I lived in an international community, my professors and fellow students coming from many different parts of the world.

Our life was primarily monastic and strictly disciplined. Our lectures were in Latin, though after a reasonably short time most of us became proficient in Italian, the official language of the community. For those interested in further study there was always the opportunity of learning other languages. We had to mix with the other students, whether we could speak their language or not, and through this initially difficult contact we soon learned a great deal of the social, political and religious conditions of many countries in the world. It was a most useful experience and prevented the development of any kind of narrow nationalism. We achieved a kind of world understanding and a sense of world concern. This was not all. The very international quality of Rome itself had an immense formative value in our lives.

The years 1933–1939, which I spent as a student in Rome, were crucial in the life of Central Europe. They were the years of Fascism and Nazism at their peak. The most indelible memory I have of that time is of the bitter tension that existed between the Fascist State and the Catholic Church. The Pope was vilified and obedience to the Church was denounced. We who walked, dressed as clerics, in the streets were apt to be shoved off the pavement by roaming gangs of Fascist youths. The walls were plastered with party propaganda at every turn. One could not only see but hear the official war cry everywhere: 'Viva Mussolini'. 'Good old Mussolini'. The whole population, brainwashed by government-controlled press and radio, became a complacent herd. Men who should have known better put their principles in their pockets and became grovelling sycophants. From their very earliest schooldays children's minds were manipulated into State-worship and to the worship of 'good old Mussolini'. They were called for Balilla drill on Sunday mornings precisely at the time when they should have been at Mass.

While all this was going on, we knew of Catholics and other Christians who defied the law and hid their Jewish neighbours to prevent their being liquidated or imprisoned by a racist régime. During those years we suffered even hunger as the result of the grim economic sanctions. Money had to be found for the Abyssinian campaign and for the brief glorification of the 'sawdust Caesar', who celebrated his imitation triumph when it was over. During all this time I had as my Superior a saintly German Carmelite who kept us informed of the equal tragedy taking place in his own country. He warned us that as future priests it would be our work to promote God's justice on earth if we were to be authentic representatives of Christ. He insisted that the teaching of the Church was essentially personal; that its centre was the human person with all his rights, and that was the key to the understanding of all man's social and political rights.

Over and over again he warned us that the age of martyrdom would never leave the Church, and that some of us might even be called to enjoy that privilege. Some of those listening had just escaped death at the hands of the Communists in the Spanish civil war. There were others in the class for whom the future held a much graver fate. Two of my companions were to die behind the Russian lines. Two others spent years in Dachau under Hitler. When he came to Rome we experienced the thrill of engaging in the conflict at close quarters. The Pope refused to see him and ordered the Vatican to be closed. In protest at his coming no one of our community went outside the doors of the college so that we should not even appear to welcome him. We would not risk being seen to be guilty by even the slightest association. We smiled with satisfaction when we heard of the powerless Palatine Guard with its antiquated musketry being drawn up outside the Vatican to prevent the entry of the armed might of the two dictators. 'Heil Hitler'. 'Good old Hitler'. 'Viva Mussolini'. 'Good old Mussolini' echoed all around us.

About that time the powerful arm of Fascism reached right into the college and deported out of the country after forty-eight hours' notice our Professor of Theology. Later on in Holland another Carmelite, the Rector of the Catholic University of Nijmegen, would be punished for his loyalty to principle. He had been appointed by the Dutch Bishops as their representative to press and radio, and when Hitler ordered him to use these means at his disposal to print and broadcast Nazi propaganda he chose to obey God rather than man and defied the might of the dictator. With that his fate was assured. He was dragged to Dachau and died there rather than betray his conscience and serve the State. He has been my hero.

All during the time of this tragedy of Europe, the Church, through its supreme authority, defended freedom of conscience and the natural rights of man against totalitarian Fascism, Nazism, Soviet Communism and the Mexican régime of 1917–1937. The teaching left an indelible impression on me and warned me for the rest of my life against the danger of State worship or the worship of political leaders. In 1937 I was ordained priest and completed my studies in 1938, when I received a Licentiate in Theology and left Rome to return to Ireland.

The Carmelite authorities in Rome wished me to return for doctoral studies, but in Ireland there was need of a teacher in my own college, and I was appointed there. I remained on the staff of the college until 1946. During that time I returned to University College, Dublin, and studied for a Higher Diploma in Education, which I obtained in 1939. In my special field of English Literature I worked for two years on a major thesis on one of the metaphysical poets and as a result was awarded an Honours Masters Degree in 1942.

Meanwhile, in my anxiety to be involved in more priestly work, I spent many of my weekends working at a hostel for 'down-and-out' men in the city of Dublin. I also coached rugby in the college, was involved in the production of a series of radio broadcast programmes of a religious nature for three years, and was also a founder member of Ireland's greatest choral society, which had as its director for many years Sir John Barbirolli. I was kept fully occupied.

In 1946 I volunteered to go to Southern Rhodesia, as it then was, to start mission work there under the then Bishop Chichester, and was appointed to lead a group of three priests who arrived in this country in

November just thirty years ago. My first appointment was to Triashill Mission, Inyanga, and in and around Inyanga I remained as a missionary until 1950, when I became parish priest in Umtali. In 1953, having been joined in the interim by numbers of other Carmelite priests from Ireland, most of the province of Manicaland was, by agreement with Bishop Chichester, separated from his jurisdiction and put under my own control as Prefect Apostolic. This state of affairs continued until 1957, when Pope Pius XII constituted the area a Diocese and appointed me as its first Bishop.

It is a significant fact that when devising a motto for my episcopate I chose the Latin phrase *Ut placeam Deo*; 'That I may please God'. I so intended these words to be a programme of action for me that on the day of my consecration, during a luncheon in honour of the occasion, and in the presence of such distinguished political figures as the late Lord Malvern and the then Prime Minister, Mr Garfield Todd, I spoke of my motto and of my determination to live it through to the utmost, and I ended my speech by saying: "As long as I am spared to rule this diocese I hope I shall please God, not men."

THE DIOCESE DEVELOPS

I come to the development of the diocese. When I first came to Rhodesia in 1946, Bishop Chichester, whose jurisdiction included all of Manicaland, pointed out to me that the work of the Church in the Eastern districts had been very much neglected and that he expected the missionaries who came with me to make up for the time lost. The Jesuit Fathers had been unable to expand because so many of them were on active service during World War II. In the whole of Manicaland in 1946 there were only six priests and three lay brothers of my Church. Their average age at that time must have been well over sixty. There were three established Mission stations, about twenty-five primary schools for Africans in the tribal trust lands under the guidance of the Church, and a junior school for European girls in Umtali – nothing more.

It was my job, therefore, either personally or vicariously through the missionaries whom I might be able to recruit, to establish the Catholic Church from one end of Manicaland to the other, that is from Inyanga North to Mahenya country at the junction of the Sabi and the Lundi. This meant first of all making friendly contact with the people, obtaining the good will of the local chiefs and the official permission of the civil authority for the establishment of those works of charity and religion which brought to the African people the Church as a living entity, making present to them the healing, educating and liberating mission of Christ.

There was always the problem of recruiting missionary personnel, priests, brothers, nuns and lay workers, and of ensuring that among them there should be professionally qualified people, teachers, doctors, nurses, etc., who could satisfy the requirements of the State. Such dedicated people were not to be found in Rhodesia, so, as the ecclesiastical authority responsible, I had to seek abroad in countries as far afield as Germany, Holland, England, Ireland, Scotland, Canada, Australia and the United States for volunteers, prepared to leave their homes and dedicate their lives to the building up of the Christian faith in Rhodesia.

This was not all. Money had to be found almost entirely from outside Rhodesia. The local European Catholic population was never more than ten per cent of the total, and their financial contribution was scarcely enough to support each – as it was then – white parish. The African population, living in a subsistence economy, gave what it could, but found it hard to understand why it should be expected to maintain missionaries completely out of its penury.

To obtain finance for Church development, the Church in Manicaland depended on the generosity of the Holy See, on Catholic communities in Europe and in the United States, and on the efforts which I made personally in preaching and lecturing tours which brought me to many countries and involved very exhausting work. It is safe to say that in the past thirty years my missionaries and I have brought into Rhodesia for Church development not less than $6 million. It has all come from abroad, as have the people involved.

The institutions which have been set up have been an irreplaceable asset to Rhodesia, and I venture to say cannot be kept in existence by the State should the support, either in finance or human resources, be withdrawn. To give one example only, I hear it stated authoritatively that at this moment in Rhodesia eighty-five per cent of the population is being served medically by only eighty-five doctors. I wonder who would work to control disease, especially in the Tribal Trust Lands, if it were not for missionaries of all denominations who work so selflessly there and in such difficult conditions.

In short, Rhodesia itself provided neither the money nor the missionaries for the establishment or expansion of the Church in its own country. It was completely dependent on everything from abroad. Unhappily this situation remains unchanged, for all practical purposes, as far as the European population is concerned. African vocations, both to the priesthood and to the sisterhoods, are steadily on the increase, and give great promise of becoming self-sufficient before the end of the century.

In the course of the last thirty years under my direction my fellow missionaries have established in the Diocese of Umtali the following institutions for the benefit of Rhodesia:

1. Between sixty and seventy primary schools, most of which have, in recent years, been ceded without any recompense to local Councils.
2. Eleven Central Mission Stations, each with its own dispensary, school, and its own group of orphans.
3. Six F1 schools, that is African academic schools going up to Form four.
4. Three FII schools – African secondary technical schools.
5. One teachers' training college in Chiduku Reserve.

6. One Nursing Assistants' Training School at Nyamaropa Reserve.
7. Regina Coeli Hospital with one hundred and ten beds in Nyamaropa.
8. A tuberculosis hospital in Umtali with one hundred beds established at the request of the local authorities because they could not cope with their then existing facilities with the number of tubercular patients. We have been running that place for the last twenty years.
9. Moreover I have established eight rural hospitals at Mission stations with an average of forty-four beds. Four of these small hospitals receive no government aid whatsoever.

Besides these institutions the Diocese of Umtali, during my episcopate, established other institutions of benefit to the country such as Marymount College, a secondary school for girls which, unfortunately, is soon to close because of the deteriorating political situation; and Carmel College, an inter-racial school for boys which has already closed down for the same reason.

During the same time the Diocese built a Minor Seminary near Melsetter for aspirants to the priesthood, and in another place a Novitiate for African Sisters. The building of places of worship has kept pace with the natural extension of the Catholic religion, and again, chiefly owing to money brought into Rhodesia from benefactors overseas, we have been able to build between twenty-five and thirty smaller churches in the Diocese, as well as the Cathedral in Umtali.

I mention this to show that my missionaries and I have not been idle during our years in Rhodesia. Whether Rhodesia approves of this activity or not, at least no one can deny that all this development has provided employment and in other ways has done no harm whatsoever to the economy of the country. Certainly we cannot be accused of sponging on Rhodesia, or of growing wealthy as a result of our labours. Not one single missionary retains a cent of any of the emoluments received from any source. All is ploughed back into the work of the Church and for the benefit of this country.

Since we are especially concerned in this court with a Mission hospital and with medicines and nurses, I would like very briefly to indicate the services provided by the Church throughout the Diocese, for example, last year, 1975. These figures have been provided through the good offices of the organisation called The Association of Rhodesian Church Hospitals, an interdenominational body, which deals with the hospitals of all denominations.

In 1975, my Diocese and its ten Mission hospitals, stretching from Inyanga North to Chisumbanje, had 559 beds. It treated in that year, 13,281 in-patients and 50,386 out-patients, while 2,192 births are recorded. The cost to the State was exactly $62,124,57. The cost to the Diocese, to me, which my missionaries and I obtained from overseas, was $76,970,95. This is small compared with what is done in other Dioceses.

I mention this to show that even if the modest contribution to public health which my Diocese makes to Rhodesia were withdrawn by the return to their home countries of our nursing sisters, the loss to Rhodesia would be very serious indeed.

No less serious in another field of activity of immense value to Rhodesia would be the closing down of all Church schools of whatever kind. I am proud of what, in the name of the Church, I have been able to provide in the realm of education for children of all races during my thirty years in Rhodesia, just as I am proud in the same cause of having been able to promote the Church's ministry of healing and aid to the sick and infirm. It is this knowledge that enables me to bear with equanimity the remarks published in the *Umtali Post* some months ago: 'There is a certain prelate living not far from here who has done more harm to Rhodesia than all the terrorists put together'. My old Professors of Philosophy, knowing the facts, would have passed their own sober Latin judgment on such an accusation, and would have said: *Disputatur inter Auctores*; 'That is a disputed question'.

Briefly, my contention is this: The work the Church does in Umtali Diocese is too valuable to jeopardise. Its continuance depends on the ability of the Bishop to recruit personnel from overseas and to find the money to keep the various institutions going. Government subsidies are minimal. Should relations between Church and State in this country deteriorate, should Rhodesia continue to reflect to the outside world a racist character, inimical to the Gospel teaching of seeing Christ in one's fellow-man, no matter how underdeveloped or physically repulsive or bodily ill, then it would be impossible to attract missionaries of any Christian creed to come to Rhodesia and the protestations of the Government about preserving Christianity and Western civilisation will be proved to be merely words. Words signifying nothing.

Worst of all, should missionaries be by law constrained to violate conscience and to be seen to collaborate with an administration which does not mete out even-handed justice to all in every field of human activity, then Christianity itself would be brought into disrepute and the way laid open for atheistic Communism.

PASTORAL TEACHING

I come to my pastoral teaching. When I was consecrated Bishop in 1957, my earlier experience of racist ideology in Europe, my training in social ethics and, by that time, my nine years of living in Rhodesia, working mostly among the African people, made me see more clearly the disabilities they suffered. In spite of the advances which they had made through their own initiative, the devoted service of all the Christian Churches, and the co-operation of an increasingly liberal civil administration, they were still marginal to society, still offered only crumbs from the privileged white man's table, still with no real and effective share in economic, political, cultural or social life. Even in the life of the Church the African seemed to be regarded patronisingly and as a second-class member. I recall my own shock when I discovered that in our city churches African Catholics were not normally admitted into the body of the church but had to worship from the sacristy, segregated from the rest of what we ought to have recognised as the one community of faith, of worship and of common Christian concern.

This fact, more than anything else, drove me to a realisation of the disparity that existed between our preaching and our practice. It made clear to me the dullness and superficial quality of our living; our unquestioning acceptance of a situation based on unchristian principles, on a racist ethic; our insensitivity to the conditions of the local indigenous people. Not only – as I recently stated in my Open Letter to the Rhodesian Government – were they marginal to society, but they were likely to remain so. Not that the then civil administration was consciously racist: it simply took for granted as 'the accepted thing', without attempting to analyse the consequences, that in Southern Rhodesia there were different moral standards applicable to the 'superior' and the 'inferior' peoples – standards which enabled the 'advanced' classes to have an easy conscience while making the 'inferior' classes an object of exploitation.

In 1958, a year after my consecration as Bishop, I preached for the first time in the Catholic Cathedral in Salisbury to a multi-racial congregation, including the Vatican representative to Southern Africa, representatives of the Government and members of the Diplomatic Corps, and clearly expressed my ideas on the need for the abolition of racism if we were really to be true to Christ's command to do unto others as we would be done by ourselves, and if we were ever going to be able to lay the foundations of a stable society in Southern Rhodesia.

In the months that followed I set to work on the theme, and finally produced a fairly extensive Pastoral Letter entitled *Purchased People*, addressed to my own diocesans and published on 29 June 1959.

The document had little effect in Rhodesia, but was immediately noticed outside the country. I understand it has been translated into 15 languages. Copies were ordered by the United Nations, and extracts appeared in translation in many countries. The Italian journal of sociological studies *Aggiornamenti Sociali* published the document *in toto*.

I had just begun my episcopate and was, as it were, the new boy in the Bishop's Conference. My

Pastoral Letter clearly shows how seriously I considered my office. I quote from it:

'Preach, a bishop must, not permitting himself to be silenced by merely human fears or temporal considerations; not watering down his message for the sake of spurious peace, or loss of friendship with any worldly authority, or possibility of being deliberately misinterpreted by wicked men . . . There are some', I said, 'who would confine all church activity to the sacristy, demanding of the Church the subservience of silence in all public affairs. Yet . . . it is precisely such people who most bitterly and vociferously condemn the Church for failing to influence our modern life'.

'States', I said, 'may persistently disregard or repudiate the rights of the spiritual power, rejecting its tutelage and claiming in their blindness absolute sovereignty, but whether they like it or not, the Church must insist on her imprescriptible right to intervene in temporal matters in so far as these affect the spiritual order of salvation, for example, the denouncing or avoiding of sin, the preservation of the order established by God, or the maintenance of her own liberty'.

One can immediately recognise in all this the influence of my experience of the totalitarian states' oppression of the Church in Central and Eastern Europe.

Continuing to explain the current problem of race relations, and attempting to show how it was at its roots a religious problem to be solved only when men recognise their common brotherhood in God, I stated: 'Once religion goes from public life, society loses its vitality and social decay sets in; law itself becomes a lawless thing; legal positivism takes the place of divine ordinance; public men forget that they are responsible to God for their official actions and confusion becomes inevitable.

'Our Divine Lord's doctrine of justice and charity can alone provide the basis for mutual understanding and peace (in Rhodesia) . . . That doctrine has in other ages proved successful in reconciling the varied social conditions of men, has civilised barbarous races, has made clear how master and servant can live in the peace of the one great Christian family'.

I continued: 'Such is the tragedy of the world's forgetfulness of God that men look down on, and treat with contempt, and persecute, and deny ordinary justice to their fellow men and continue to call themselves Christians'.

Blaming much of the disorder on the neglect of Natural Law, I said: 'Wherever the genius of law seeks out its origins, there it will find Natural Law', and added: 'Wherever, as here in Central Africa, it is neglected, grave injustices are inflicted and prolonged on whole groups of people, family life is disrupted, the liberty of the individual is needlessly constrained, uninstructed masses are confused about what is their duty and what is their due, and legislators themselves, with no very clear idea of the essential nature of man or of his destiny, and with no unalterable principles to guide them enact measures so ill-considered and immature that they make a mockery of justice itself '.

Next in this Pastoral Letter I dealt briefly with the crucial problem of African nationalism which was then revealing itself in all its complexity throughout Rhodesia. I said: 'The desire of a national group to be free from subjection to a foreign ruler is a most legitimate one, provided it can be achieved without any violation of justice'.

Pleading for a change of outlook on the part of extremists on both African and European sides, I said that a vocal minority of Europeans was responsible for much of the ill-feeling which exists. 'This minority', I said, 'basing its cause on the plea that control of the country must always remain in the hands of civilised persons, perverts that excellent sentiment into meaning that one race of people, their own, shall dominate for all time and at any cost', and I added: 'The treasured belief that they are courageous, confident, virile, fair-minded and adventurous people must surely be dismissed as an illusion if the Europeans of this country are not prepared or are incapable of moderating their outlook to meet the challenge of a changing world in which the barriers of space and time have so rapidly been broken down that men of different racial origins are brought more quickly and closely together than ever before'.

I wrote that nearly twenty years ago. It seems still appropriate today.

I have devoted a good deal of time to describing this document, because I wish to indicate the character of my criticism of the national scene. The same style of philosophical argument pervades all the statements of the Catholic Bishops of Rhodesia in the years that followed, because I played some considerable part in framing them.

Unfortunately the people of this country either did not take the trouble to study what the other Bishops and I had to say, lest perhaps their conscience be disturbed, or maybe because the sober philosophical argument was beyond their comprehension.

The result of all this was that I acquired a reputation of being simply a trouble-maker, a political agitator who was, as the Irish are alleged to be, just against the Government for the heck of it. I was written off, as one clerical visitor to Rhodesia put it to an appreciative public last year, as 'a lovable lunatic, who really should not be listened to or allowed to remain in the country at all'.

Such an opinion was formalised some years later by the Chichester Club, a society of Catholic business and professional men in Salisbury who, in fact, made an official request to Pope Paul to have me removed from the office of Bishop of Umtali.

My Pastoral Letter of 1959 was followed by a similar instruction to all the Catholics of Rhodesia two years later and signed by all the Bishops of this country. The theme was clearly expressed in the title: *Peace through Justice*. It was an effort to ensure that the Church should be seen to advocate a cessation to the disturbances that took place throughout the country at the time when a new Constitution for the country was being framed.

From 1962 to 1965 I was almost totally concerned with that historic event which was the Second Vatican Council held at Rome during those years, and attended by all the Catholic Bishops of the world. Over one hundred years had passed since there had been such a gathering. The aim of the Council was the reform of the Church in every aspect of its activity where reform was necessary, and a renewal of its own understanding of its mission in the world.

Although I was completely unknown in such a distinguished gathering, in the first session I received almost one thousand votes and was elected a member of the important Secretariat for the Promotion of Christian Unity, a group of twenty-four Cardinals and Bishops whose objective was to make contact with the heads of other Christian denominations in the hope that through studying our differences and achieving mutual understanding we might possibly, in time to come, achieve corporate unity.

Once again the experience of four years working in an international atmosphere, meeting intelligent and disciplined men from every corner of the globe, influenced my understanding of world affairs and made me realise that there was emerging in history a planetary unity of mankind and a notion of international community. The contrast with the parochial, morally primitive and racist existence of Rhodesia provided a revelation and a shock from which I have never recovered.

In the Second Session of the Council during 1963 I delivered my first speech in Latin to the Bishops assembled in St Peter's Basilica in Rome. Looking back on it now, it is interesting to note that it was a denunciation of racism as it had been applied to the first people of God, the Jews.

As a member of the Unity Secretariat, I was involved every day with the most intelligent minds of the Church in framing documents which were afterwards approved as bearing the most authoritative character for Catholics all over the world. We were blessed too with the aid of all other Churches and with lay experts from many nations. My particular Secretariat was especially concerned with the framing of the historic Declaration on Religious Liberty, a declaration on Anti-Semitism, and an extremely important Decree on Ecumenism.

Here again the seminal ideas of religious liberty and racism, with their correlative problems of the relationship between Church and State and the rights of racial groups and religious and political minorities, matured in my mind and much influenced my thinking in relation to Rhodesia.

In 1964 I achieved some international notoriety for an important address to the Council delivered in Latin to the 2,300 Bishops in which I criticised proposed legislation about the Church's missionary activity, and by my intervention I managed to have the proposals rejected and a new document substituted. In the following, final year of the Council I was chosen to address the gathering in the name of all the Church's missionary Orders when the definite document on mission endeavour was voted and approved.

I mention this particularly because the document seemed to have the official approval of the Holy See and was presented to the assembled Bishops as having that character. In spite of that, I recognised that as a loyal son of the Church I had not only the freedom to object to it, but even the duty to do so. I understood that it would be an act of disloyalty not to say, and to say fearlessly, what I considered to be wrong with the document.

I mention this to illustrate the fact that in criticising the State of Rhodesia I am not behaving as an enemy, but rather as a responsible citizen, and it is in this attitude that I persist to this day.

My learned counsel have encouraged me to give all these details of my activity, possibly to refute the opinion held by many of my critics in this country that I am simply an irresponsible trouble-maker with no understanding whatsoever of the grave issues affecting this country, and possibly one who would have no hesitation in promoting violence or encouraging Communism. At best I am dismissed by many simply as a talkative 'do-gooder' who has no intention of remaining permanently in Rhodesia and who would leave the country and fly to safety elsewhere should danger ever arise.

In regard to this latter accusation which, indeed, has been made many times, I might say that I have never been dispossessed of my passport. The authorities have paid me the compliment of presuming that I would do nothing so dishonourable as running away, even when faced with this trial and its serious consequences.

For the other supposition that I am simply a 'do-gooder' with no logical reason for my rejection of racism, may I here make explicit my belief that unless a man has cultivated in himself a contemplative mind, unless his life is characterised by inwardness, by an appreciation of his own identity, by an understanding that he is not mass-produced, but purpose-made, that his possession of intellect and will prove to him that he has been called into existence by Someone – not just by Some Thing, by some blind cosmic force – unless a man realises all this profoundly in his own heart and recognises that such is the condition, the privilege of existence of every other human being, no matter what his race or colour or condition or creed, unless he realises precisely this, he can have no solid foundation for his denunciation of racism and must be prepared to be described as a mere 'do-gooder'.

My rejection of the evil of racism is founded, I believe, on such a contemplative conclusion and is supported by the Gospel of Christ as clearly expressed in St Matthew's Gospel. Christ wishes to be served and to be seen in the most abject and neglected of his fellow men. This should be taught and practised by all who profess to follow him.

I think of an Anglican priest missionary, known throughout the length and breadth of Rhodesia,

Father Arthur Shearly Cripps, who, with the vision of a very special grace, saw Christ in this way in his fellow man, in his black African servant, and who wrote:

> Oh, happy eyes are mine
> That pierce the black disguise
> And see Our Lord!
> Oh, woe of woes!
> That I should see, that I should know
> Whom 'tis they use that use Him so!

The years following the Vatican Council were crucial as far as my attitude to the problems of Rhodesia were concerned. I was now able to recognise, as never before, how the rights of human persons were being systematically violated in many countries and communities. Some of these rights, though thankfully not all of them, were violated in Rhodesia, yet no one recognised them, or if so, dared to protest against them, though Rhodesia claimed to have declared its political independence in the name of God and for the preservation of Christianity and Western Civilisation.

Recognition of this widespread moral malaise inspired the Catholic Church to convene a Synod of its Bishops in Rome in 1971 to examine the whole problem and search for solutions based on a firm and radical conviction that it is God's will that justice be done on earth, that therefore the Church cannot remain indifferent to the deplorable state of affairs which existed throughout the world to the widespread neglect of justice, both in the profession of law and in the practice of politics.

I had the privilege of representing the Bishops of Rhodesia at that Synod, and I carried out my duty of illustrating to the assembled prelates the racist character of our society, both in political, social, economic and cultural life. It was at the meeting that I coined the phrase which has since passed into common use to describe our political structure. I said: "Rhodesia is a political absurdity. It is a State without a nation".

The official document published at the end of the Synod and entitled *Justice in the World* clearly stated the obligation imposed by conscience and by the Christian faith on all who professed that faith to take positive action to promote justice in the world and to work through peaceful means for the dismantling of those unjust structures which denied other human beings integral human development. This directive is summed up in the following magisterial sentence from the document: 'Action on behalf of justice and participation in the transformation of the world fully appear to us, the Bishops, as a constitutive dimension of the preaching of the Gospel, or, in other words, of the Church's mission for the redemption of the human race and its liberation from every oppressive situation.'

After such a clear indication of where my duty lay, how could I, or any other Bishop, for that matter, remain indifferent to the gross injustice which existed all around me and which especially had to be borne by the vast majority of the Rhodesian population? Pope Paul himself made explicit what should be done. It would not be enough, he said, just to publish statements pointing out and denouncing injustice wherever it might be found. Positive and prophetic action ought to be taken, the lead ought to be given by the Church if it is to maintain any shadow of credibility in its mission.

These are his words: "It is not enough to recall principles, state intentions, point to crying injustices and utter prophetic denunciations. These words will lack real weight unless they are accompanied for each individual by a livelier awareness of personal responsibility and by effective action."

This ought to explain much of my activity here in Rhodesia in my work for the promotion of a sane order and the eradication of injustices in any shape or form. It was a work inspired by Christian teaching and based on the belief that peace can only be achieved where justice is sought, protected and practised.

In all my criticism there was nothing whatsoever of a spirit of anarchy. I had experienced in my young manhood the tragedies of state absolutism, of blind following of political figures. I was convinced that the old moral and paternalistic concept of the State should be replaced by a juridical and constitutional one in which the true subject of politics is the human person, the citizen. I believed that it was morally wrong and pregnant with danger for the future of Rhodesia to banish the majority population, the African people, to the fringe of society, to deny them the right of self-determination and independence. I held as fundamental for the pursuit of lasting peace that power, responsibility and decision-making should be shared by all who could reasonably take part in it, and that these activities should not be the monopoly of one group or race segment of the people. I understood that democracy, to fulfil its true functions, requires an aristocracy of mind and character, and that neither one element nor the other, nor indeed both were the exclusive possession of the ruling white minority in Rhodesia. With St Thomas Aquinas I knew well that not all citizens have either the will or the capacity to concern themselves with politics, but that in practice any good form of government ought to incorporate the democratic principle.

Above all I detested and denounced at every possible opportunity the use of violence, whether the institutional violence created and made respectable by parliamentary legislation, or the brutal, physical violence which is more easily recognised, but no less detestable.

As far back as my Pastoral Letter of 1959 I had stated that any organised attempt to overthrow a legally constituted government can only be justified by the presence of the following conditions:

1. If there be on the part of the government grave and prolonged violation of the rights of the subject;
2. If all constitutional methods of obtaining redress have been seriously tried and have failed;
3. If there be a reasonable prospect of success and of setting up an objectively better government; because, as I said, unless there be, the common good demands that civil war be averted.

I would like to point out here that at no time in my life have I ever taken part in party politics. Even now, after thirty years in Rhodesia, I know hardly any of the prominent political leaders. I stand apart from them and prefer it that way. 'The changing of unjust and oppressive social structures, and hence planned and organised action in the political field, is mainly the task of the laity, because the political field is their proper field of action. The priest normally should not involve himself in ideological and partisan disputes, since this would jeopardise his function as a mediator and would possibly tarnish the purity of his message and indeed his freedom as a representative of the Church'.

In 1970 I was elected President of the Rhodesia

Catholic Bishops' Conference, and held that office for two years. It was during that time that I strenuously opposed the recognition of the Land Tenure Act, which would have made it impossible for the Church to be faithful to its mandate to treat all human beings as equal members of the one family of God through creation and redemption. At a meeting of all the Bishops and the heads of all the religious Orders working in this country, I proposed that we should close all our institutions, all our schools, hospitals, orphanages, homes for the aged – everything – rather than be false to the principle which we preached as the fundamental tenet of our faith, namely that we call God 'Our Father', that we must do to others as we would like to be done by ourselves, that we must try to see Christ in our fellow man – the hungry, the thirsty, the naked, the stranger, the prisoner. Above all, I argued, we must say with the same resolution as the first Christians: 'We must obey God rather than men.'

The government has been prudent enough to let our decision and its consequences go unchallenged. The contribution made by all the Christian Churches and ecclesiastical communities to the life of the nation has been so widespread and beneficial that were they to be forced to close down their institutions rather than be false to principle, the loss to Rhodesia would be enormous.

Certainly it seems that the government appeared by this to recognise that the Christian Church in Rhodesia could not continue to exist if, because of the colour of a person's skin, or his racial origin, it could be forced to refuse its mission of healing or of educating to any human being who came to our hospitals or schools and requested the service of charity which the Church professes to offer in the name of its founder. By taking no action, when the Church did not observe the law as laid down in the Land Tenure Act, the State seemed to indicate that it gave due and proper recognition to the primacy of conscience.

In the past five or six years, as everyone knows, restrictive legislation has been greatly increased and today has reached unbelievable proportions. The growth in African nationalist consciousness and political activity, both within and outside Rhodesia's borders, has largely been responsible for it. Particularly the monolithic fracture of the Portuguese colonial empire has been instrumental in bringing into existence African nationalist parties whose aim is the overthrow of the present government of Rhodesia and the setting up of another administration based on black majority rule.

The determination of both sides to the struggle not to give in has brought Rhodesia to a state of war and has given reason for the daily increase in oppressive legislation. The machinery of coercion is multiplied and legalised without any apparent end to it in sight. Wherever such a condition of affairs obtains, it is symptomatic of serious social disorder. Wherever the civil state is well ordered and firmly established on the consent of the people, the machinery of coercion should not obtrude itself on the notice of the citizens.

Unhappily, this is not so in Rhodesia, and as a result the Catholic Commission for Justice and Peace has had increasingly to concern itself with the proliferation of acts of violence brought to its attention by the general public, almost entirely by the African population, in her effort to obtain redress through a legitimate Church authority.

I have had the honour of being President of the Rhodesia Justice and Peace Commission for the past two years. The majority of its members are young Europeans, professional men, who, with their African fellows, give unlimited time and expert attention to the searching out of acts of injustice and the obtaining of redress or compensation. It is a joy for me to report that although the Commission acts under the aegis of the Catholic Bishops' Conference, its members belong to different Christian denominations and sometimes to none. The work of the Commission has at various times been greatly supported by the heads of other Churches, particularly when it has had to make representations to Government requesting a public inquiry into some of the more serious matters brought to its attention by complainants who had no other help available.

Sad to say, the response of the State to these appeals made by responsible people for the investigation of injustices has not been what might have been expected from an administration which not only claims to be democratic, but which actually proclaims that it is the defender of Christianity and Western Civilisation. In spite of all the appeals and personal approaches made to the Government, no independent inquiry into allegations of brutality has yet been carried out. Instead, abuse of the most bitter and defamatory type has been heaped on the Commission and its members from all parts of the country, by Government supporters in Parliament and out of it, by a cowardly and sycophantic Press, and above all by the State-controlled and manipulated television and broadcasting systems.

It is history, well recorded, both in the Press and in Hansard at the time, how the Justice and Peace Commission's charges, compiled with meticulous

53

and professional skill and published in the pamphlet *The Man in the Middle*, were rejected without examination, and how people like me, who were associated in the preparation of the document, were reviled, both in the House of Assembly and in the Senate.

And so, instead of accepting the challenge to investigate and thus manifest a proper concern that justice should be done and be seen to be done, the security of the House of Assembly and of the Senate was used to attack the Commission and defame its members.

However, out of such attacks much good eventually came. The African people, whose grievances we had attempted to present to the authorities in a responsible manner, and for whom we sought justice, now recognised that there were in the country some people, surprisingly to them, even Europeans, who were concerned on their behalf, and as a result the racial tensions, which were daily increasing in the densely populated townships, were relaxed, and the suffering people felt that someone at least was speaking on their behalf. The Justice and Peace Commission acted as a relief valve for the pent-up emotions of the black people, made marginal in their own country, and it thus provided a service of extremely great value to Rhodesia.

Not only that. The Commission's work quite categorically offset the propaganda of those who tried to enlist the African population of Rhodesia to Communism. The Christian Church, as represented by the efforts of the Commission, was seen to be the support of the under-privileged, the advocate of the voiceless, the tireless defender of the rights of the human person, the friend of the disenfranchised masses. That was perfectly clear to great numbers of the young African intelligentsia who otherwise, in their unhappy condition, might easily have been swayed by the Communist cry that the Christian Church will not stir a finger to help the underdog, but simply preaches pious platitudes to him, counsels him to be even more long-suffering, not to challenge the privileged few who manipulate him for their own selfish gain, and that whatever the hardships of this life, it would be all made right in the next; there would be pie in the sky when you die.

Having personally received much of the abuse from Cabinet Ministers and members of the Senate – from their seat of safety – because of my being President of the Justice and Peace Commission, I was on one notable occasion last year delighted to be able to use, on behalf of the Church, one of the more scurrilous attacks made on us by the then Minister of Justice, Law and Order. It is appropriate to my argument that I should record the incident.

I was invited to an important conference in Bonn in November of last year, sponsored by the Justice and Peace Commission of West Germany. The purpose of the conference was to find out how the Christian West could best assist the newly independent African nations so as to wean them away from the advances of Communism. At one point during the formal discussions at the conference table, one of the 16 African ambassadors complained that the Christian West had been silent for many years, and had connived, by its silence, in benefiting by the exploitation of the masses in the colonies. I jumped at this opportunity to reply, and produced from my briefcase the front page of *The Rhodesia Herald*, which carried the headline: 'Church acts as Fifth Column', an accusation made some time earlier in the House of Assembly by the Minister for Justice, Law and Order.

In the widespread denunciation of the Justice and Peace Commission, the media of communication in Rhodesia used all the means at their disposal to bring the Commission, and me, its President, into disrepute so as to nullify all our efforts. Nothing was too despicable to be attempted. In the Senate, not only did a Senator Chief propose that I should be removed, but a hitherto highly respected Senator Chairman of the Senate Legal Committee defamed me in the Chamber by asserting that I exercised a dictatorial influence in the Commission and appointed and dismissed its Chairman as I thought fit. Such an accusation made in the Senate by a man who bore an honourable name I found intolerable, and through the medium of the national Press I challenged him to substantiate or refute his defamatory remark. To this day he has refused to accept the challenge. It seems that defamation of my character from the safe sanctuary of the Senate is justifiable, according to Rhodesian standards.

I cannot too greatly emphasise the need for the Church to be seen here and now as a courageous voice in the denunciation of acts of injustice, particularly those felt by the African people, and as a committed and active agent in the peaceful dismantling of unjust social structures wherever they exist. Such clear-cut and public denunciation and action is especially necessary when we are told that Communists threaten the whole of Southern Africa, and that all along the Eastern border, that is all along my Diocese, the forces of Marxism are already at work to invade and take over Rhodesia.

I must say at once that personally I doubt every bit of government propaganda that I hear on the RBC or RTV, just as I read with the greatest sense of scepticism much that is printed in our Rhodesian newspapers. I do not believe that Rhodesian Africans want Communism, or Russia, or China, or Cuba. I believe that they want to be with the West, and with the English speaking world.

One highly gifted African of great academic distinction told me, when I asked him if his people felt any natural inclination towards Communism: "My lord, Communism is completely alien to us. Can you imagine our giving our cattle, let alone our children, to the State? We are capitalists at heart. Unfortunately we have no capital."

One way or the other, however, it is vital for the preservation of the Christian Church in this country that it be clearly seen by the underprivileged masses and by those who endeavour to attract them to Communism to be prepared to practise what it preaches, to be unpopular when need be, to stand up and suffer for the underprivileged, to be known to be opposed to all unjust agencies, no matter how powerful, and not even by fear of persecution to be terrified into the silence of complicity.

As far as I am concerned in my Diocese at this time, no Communist agent, I pray, will ever be able to accuse me or my missionaries of being indifferent to the appeal of the sick, the hungry or the naked. No Communist agent will ever be able to say that by our silence we gave consent to discrimination based on race or religion or political belief. Whatever befalls, I and those wonderful missionaries I am privileged to have with me will always try to do God's will, not men's.

In saying all this, I realise it will be claimed by the State that its very raison d'être is the preservation of Christianity and of Western civilisation. To this I reply that surely that civilisation which we now call Western, and which was once significantly called Christian, is based on effort made to achieve a social order directed towards the good of the person, on an acceptance of the fact that everyone is a person endowed with intelligence and free will, and that the human person is and must be the source, subject and goal of all its social institutions.

The philosophical principle here enunciated finds little acceptance in the thinking of those who rule Rhodesia. Neither would they, in practice, agree to the assertion that all men and nations enjoy the right to development regarded as a dynamic interpretation of all those fundamental human rights on which the aspirations of individuals and nations are based, which includes the right to equal opportunities in the cultural, civic, social and economic spheres, and to an equitable distribution of the natural resources. Such doctrine is utterly at variance with what obtains in practice, and is sanctified by legislation in this so-called bastion of Western civilisation.

As for our being a free Christian society at all, I doubt it very much. The very racist ethic which is the fount of all our discriminatory legislation, which informs the minds of the electorate and determines the customs of the privileged ruling class is utterly alien to the mind of Christ. As I wrote in my Pastoral Message in 1959: "What is really at the heart of the trouble is that God has been banished politely from public life, His eternal law has been quietly set aside, hesitant lip-service only is paid to Him, and thoughtless men attempt to order society without taking the Maker's rules into account."

In Rhodesia, for instance, at this moment it seems that only a State-censored form of Christianity is permitted to be broadcast from RBC or RTV. Every single religious script has to be submitted, and if necessary censored by some State official before it can be delivered to the general public. This is fact, not hearsay.

One Anglican Bishop told me of the preposterous presumption of one official of the RBC who corrected his text – the Bishop's text – before it could be broadcast. One of the priests in my own Diocese had his text completely rejected. That I could understand. The good man was either so innocent or so imprudent as to think that he might be permitted to speak on our national broadcasting station on such a delicate subject as the saintly Lord Chancellor of England, Sir Thomas More, who gladly laid his head on the executioner's block to show that his first duty was to conscience and the Church, that he had first to serve God, and only then, if it were in accordance with God's will, to serve his King.

And this is not the only way in which it is evident that a new form or interpretation of Christianity exists in our midst and enjoys the blessing of the State.

Morality has, in many respects, been banned from public life by order of the Ministers of State and some of their subjects. This is true. I recall the order of him who until recently was Minister of Defence, an order which I challenged in the national Press and which has not been answered. The Minister told the security forces, in effect, not to hesitate to kill and destroy anyone and any place where there might be terrorists, and said that if innocent people were killed or maimed in the process, it was just too bad. It was their misfortune, not his fault. I reminded him and other members of the Government, in a letter to the Press, that political authority must always be exercised within the limits of morality, and, of course, for that, drew down upon myself the wrath of all Rhodesian white racists, with their telephone calls in the middle of the night to disturb my sleep, these brave people, their threats in the street, their unspeakably filthy letters and their drawings of abuse. Such is the penalty for presuming to suggest that morality has any place in public life.

You think this is exaggerated? May I read for you, as reported in *The Rhodesia Herald* of 30th July, 1976, the directive given by the Secretary for Law and Order to recruit patrol officers during their passing-out parade at the Morris Depot in Salisbury. He told them "not to be too squeamish in departing from the niceties of established procedures which are appropriate for more normal times". What is this but an indication by a State authority that excessive punitive measures may be exercised without fear against the general public? Is this not another indication that political authority and morality, in the mind of the State, have no natural correlation?

I very well realise that when the security of any State is threatened, extreme measures may have to be taken for the common good. But in a so-called Christian State, how does it accord with the declared principle of preserving Christian civilisation that the government has now, I understand, in a high state of preparedness, a plan for the taking over of Christian Missions of all denominations everywhere in Rhodesia?

What, for instance, is one to say of a government which claims to be Christian and which allows its officers to burst, fully armed, into a church while Mass, divine worship, is being celebrated, and order the priest to hurry up and leave the altar, chomping their rifles to intimidate him into obeying them? This happened to one of my priests at one of my Missions in my Diocese a few weeks ago, and, strange to say, I first got the news of it on the day when I read in *The Rhodesia Herald* of 25th August, 1976, of a similar case which took place in Uganda, when a Catholic priest was dragged from the altar in his church by another kind of soldiery.

Is this what one expects from the Government of Rhodesia? And when the unfortunate priest was finally locked up in a cell, and I was allowed to see him, I was shocked to the core that he, or any human being, should be housed in such appalling conditions. This was not in Uganda, or in some country of Eastern Europe. It was not in a Communist country, or in some remote South American republic, this was here in Rhodesia. It was not perpetrated by some sadist in some remote corner of Rhodesia, where no responsible authority could see it and later on protest that it was done without his approval. This was here, just beyond those walls, not twenty yards away from where we are assembled.

Let me tell you what I saw. After the lawyer whom I had employed had been refused permission to see the unfortunate priest alone, after bail had been offered and refused because no charge had been laid, through the kindness of some humane officials of the police service, I was permitted to see my brother priest. A great steel door with two bars was opened, and inside, to my horror, I saw the priest standing barefoot on a cold cement floor. His shoes and socks had been removed. His belt, his watch, his rosary had all been taken from him. In one corner, near the door, four or five narrow slats of wood battened together close to the floor made what passed for a bed. The unfortunate man had to sleep on that as if on rails. There were three blankets, but no pillow and no mattress whatsoever. In a far corner of the room a square cement block about two or two-and-a-half feet high, was built solidly into the wall. There was a hole in the centre and a pushbutton at the side. This was the toilet. To use it the prisoner had to climb up and somehow try to squat. There were two small windows very high up on the ceiling. There was no table, no chair, no stool, nothing whatsoever to sit on. Food, consisting of porridge and beans, was brought to the prisoner at six o'clock in the morning, and he had nothing more to eat until six o'clock in the evening.

Thanks to the humanity of the officer-in-charge, after some days I was permitted to send him a New Testament and a Breviary, the priest's prayerbook. But try as I could I was unable to find out when this unfortunate man might be brought to trial or how his condition might further be improved. Then, suddenly, eleven days later he was called out of his cell, given his shoes and socks and other belongings and told that he might go; that he was free.

It is safe to presume that this priest is not the only one who has had to suffer like this without any charge whatsoever being laid against him. Is this the sort of treatment one expects from civilised beings? Is this the way Christian governments with Western civilised traditions deal with their citizens who have been guilty of no crime? Is it not right that I should speak and denounce such injustice for all the world to hear, such Pharisaism, such hypocrisy?

The whole world is alerted and alarmed, and no expense is spared to seek out and recover a sophisticated instrument of war, either sunk in the ocean or hijacked in another country. But the same world is indifferent to human beings locked up and forgotten and sunk in gaols and in internment camps all over the world.

The general public knows nothing about all this, I am sure. The electorate would not believe it were it to be made known. They would not credit that the men they elected to Parliament would ever allow such things to happen.

I wrote about this general condition of affairs in an English newspaper on 3rd April of this year. 'For the most part the ordinary European does not realise that anything like this appalling system exists. He has been brain-washed by the officially-controlled media and by a subservient Press. He has heard of such things happening during the last war in Central Europe, but he will simply not believe that this happens right under his nose in Rhodesia. That a previous Prime Minister, Garfield Todd, is still under house arrest worries him not at all, neither does the daily tally of murdered Africans, shot dead merely for breaking the curfew. He is not in the least troubled at the fact that the Government censors every single radio talk given by ministers of religion, and chooses 'safe' men to be given time on the air. That no member of the parliamentary opposition is ever heard on radio or television he regards as only proper. It never occurs to him that there is anything unusual in all this. Were he to hear African Nationalists speak of the need for another Nuremberg, he probably would not see that either.'

In writing this way about such things, I believe I do a service of great value to the people of Rhodesia and to free men the world over. I believe that if this system of government be permitted to continue without any change whatsoever, without any attempt at providing equality under the law and equal opportunity for all men, then the danger of another

Nuremberg could be very real indeed.

Neither time nor numbers are on the side of those who rule us today. The moral state of the country gives little hope for the future either. We have one of the highest divorce rates in the world. Our maternity homes have been turned into geriatric units. The civil administration seems to have lost all capacity for self-examination, for self-discipline, for self-regulation, and to my mind it is heading for chaos. And still the selfish electorate, callous and insensitive to the condition of the masses, thinks it can carry on regardless.

Selfishness or avarice in men or in nations is a sure sign of moral underdevelopment. If this is true, and I believe it is, then those who rule us must be regarded by thinking men the world over as moral primitives. Yet to those who do not see beneath the surface, Rhodesia appears a haven of order and cleanliness and discipline. Yes, indeed. It is the same order, discipline and cleanliness that one finds in prison compounds and cemeteries. The good life, the power and the wealth which people in Rhodesia claim as the culmination of their so-called civilising presence in Africa, of their professional and technical achievement, divorced as it is from basic morality, must surely be regarded as nothing more than, if I may quote Toynbee in his *Study of History*: 'The opening chapters of complete decline.'

I have said that in speaking openly of these things and criticising them, no matter how unpopular these truths may be, I am doing a service to Rhodesia and its people. Anyone who loves Rhodesia and its people, anyone who wants peace here, must surely recognise that the laws which have built up and continue to maintain such national disorder must quickly be revoked by the rulers; the unjust social structures must, without delay, be dismantled. In short, institutional violence must be abolished if racial war, with the most horrible consequences, is to be avoided.

Were there to be an African Government in this country – and indeed this seems inevitable, and very soon – and if the present laws which have been enacted and applied to create and preserve privilege – if these were retained and applied in reverse against the European, what a protest there would be! For instance, only a small number of European children would be allowed to attend school, and an even smaller percentage would be permitted to pass the State examinations. Employment and access to apprenticeships would be reserved to black people only. All officers – and I believe this will change – in the Army and police would belong to the governing race. Prison sentences for Europeans could be served in cells similar to the one I have described, and with the same civilised amenities. Thousands of whites could be driven from their homes and farms without compensation and housed in the open veld behind wire fences with lights blazing all night, with limited sanitation and under curfew, as is now done with certainly at least 100,000 Africans in the so-called 'protected villages'.

But perhaps an African Government might be more considerate. Europeans might possibly be treated better than Africans were. They could even be given alternative accommodation. It might be possible to arrange for them to have at least a roof over their heads during the rainy season as many Africans had not. In Salisbury, for instance, houses in Highfields might be given in exchange for those in Highlands. With laws in force now, but applied in reverse, white people, children among them, could be arrested or restricted without trial, and any brutalities practised by the Security Forces could be withdrawn from the jurisdiction of the courts, as has been done by the application of the Indemnity and Compensation Act. Trials could be held *in camera* and sentence of death by hanging carried out without it being necessary to inform anyone, including the closest relatives, that the executions had taken place.

Should anyone feel that he could no longer live in such a country, the Departure from Rhodesia Act of 1972 could be invoked to prevent his leaving. Moreover, should he manifest in any way contempt for an officer of the State, he could be severely punished, and if under the age of eighteen, could be given a whipping, provided the whipping did not exceed eight strokes.

These are only a few of the disabilities which the African majority now suffers in Rhodesia and has had to tolerate for years 'to maintain standards', to preserve Christianity and Western civilisation. I believe that there are two notions of Christianity abroad in this country, that promoted by the official Christian missionary bodies, who have done so much for Rhodesia, and that peculiar form based on a racist blasphemy and sponsored by the Government.

Rhodesians are prepared, by their peripheral activities, to rewrite the *Guinness Book of Records* in every single endurance test, as long as they are not required to do to their neighbour what they would like done to themselves in this so-called Christian country.

THE AVILA SITUATION

Your worship and gentlemen, in the course of this next part of my unsworn statement there will be many references to the priest who has been the Superior at Avila Mission, and who has since left the country. I would like permission, instead of using his full name, and for his own security, to be permitted to refer to him as 'Father X'.

I want to tell you exactly what happened in regard to the first offence with which I am charged by the State. What I have to say is taken from my diary which I have kept with considerable detail for some years past.

On Wednesday, 21st April of 1976, I was at Regina Coeli Mission in Nyamaropa Reserve on an ordinary visit. As the Mission is situated within a very short distance of the Mozambique border, and since it comprises not only a secondary school, a large hospital and a training centre for African nurse-assistants, I was particularly anxious that things should be running smoothly and that all was well. The fact that the Mission had been cut off for some weeks by swollen rivers during the rainy season, and the further fact that it had no telephone connection with the outside world, had always given me reason for special concern. Besides the two priests at the Mission there were five Franciscan Sisters, some from Scotland and some from Ireland. I was very happy to realise during my visit that everything was proceeding normally and that the community was quite happy, although two of the

Sisters were on that particular day in Melsetter.

I drove from Regina Coeli Mission to Avila in Inyanga North on 21st April, and shortly after arrival was informed that a letter had been handed into the Mission requesting medicines. I was shown the note, and, as far as I can remember, it asked for anti-malarial tablets and medicines for diarrhoea. My recollection of the incident is that I was told that the letter had been delivered by a villager, a man, on behalf of what are in the summons called 'terrorists'. I was asked what ought to be done about it, and I replied that we ought to give medical aid to anyone who asked, and that the nurses should not argue about the matter. I have a distinct recollection of saying that as far as medical help was concerned, no missionary should inquire about the religion or politics of those who asked for help. I remember also saying that if the Security Forces came looking for medicines, they too were to be given whatever they needed and whatever the Mission could afford to give.

I realised clearly what my decision involved. It was a decision which I had arrived at long before, knowing that what had already happened in other parts of the country when terrorists came to Mission stations would, in all probability, happen in my Diocese. First of all, having thought the matter out, I realised that any request for food or medical help made a particular claim on the Church's ministry of charity, and that, were it to be refused, the Church might easily be accused of preaching one thing and doing another. I remembered Christ's words in which he reprimanded those who lacked charity and failed to see Him in the suffering poor. His words, which are known to you all, are these: 'I was hungry and you gave me not to eat, thirsty and you gave me not to drink, naked and you did not clothe me . . .', etc.

It was of paramount importance to me that the Church should not suffer in its reputation by failing in charity. In particular I realised that in nearby Mozambique the Church had suffered greatly because of its century-old association with a colonial regime, and that a Marxist ideology was now actively being promoted among the people of that country. I had heard too that this ideology was shared by those who came armed into Rhodesia determined to achieve equality under the law and equal opportunity for all the citizens of Rhodesia. It seemed vitally important to me that these people should not, on their contact with the Church in Rhodesia, be made to believe that it collaborated with the regime which they considered oppressive. Rather it was necessary for the Church, as represented by our Missions, to manifest a courageous and generous Christian concern, even for the wayward.

This was the first thing which decided my thinking in regard to the attitude to be adopted by the missionaries should they be approached by terrorists.

The second decisive motive was the safety of the personnel involved. What would happen, then, were they, few in number, without any means of defence whatever, without even a telephone closer than a two-hour journey – I did not know at the time there was a telephone at the police station – what would these helpless people do were they to refuse the things demanded of them? Certainly, from all the government propaganda that we had listened to, one could only conclude that their lives would be in imminent danger. Informers were given little mercy, we were told. We had been provided with gruesome Government agency reports of how unfortunate people, forced to inform, had been either brutally murdered or savagely mutilated by having their lips and ears cut off.

Here was my problem. If our missionaries deny the medicines, there is nothing to prevent armed men from invading the Mission at any hour of the day or night and forcibly taking what they wanted. As a matter of fact, some time later another group of armed men, Europeans this time, members of the Security Force, came to the Mission clinic, came into the premises, asked for what they wanted, were given it, and even demanded Penbriton, the most expensive drug which the Mission had, and went off. Nobody reported such an incident.

Suppose then the Mission authorities were not to inform, they were guilty of a most serious crime to which was attached the gravest punishment. Rather than have any one of my missionaries involved in such an issue, I had resolved long before, and now at Avila Mission I made my resolution clear to all the Mission staff, that I alone would be guilty of any crime involved through giving food or medical help to forbidden persons, and that I would also be responsible for the further crime of not reporting their presence. For this I stand here today. I alone am guilty. All other members of the Mission staff who acted in defiance of the law did so under obedience from me.

The person who had come looking for medicines had gone off and it was understood that a parcel containing what was requested, or as much as was available and what we could afford to give, was to be left until called for. Meanwhile the Superior of the Mission, a European priest, and the two European nursing Sisters left that very afternoon to attend a function at another convent of their Order in Marandellas. I remained on at the Mission that afternoon, and while I was out for a walk after the others had gone to Marandellas some European and African soldiers arrived at the Mission and told the African priest stationed there that a group of terrorists had robbed a store and a bus somewhere north of the Mission. I recollect nothing more of that day, but the next morning I set off for Umtali.

That afternoon, having arrived at Umtali, I was visited by the Mission doctor from Regina Coeli hospital, which is very near the border. He came with his wife and baby. The man in question had come a few months before to work at Regina Coeli hospital on a three-year contract. He seemed perfectly happy at first, but after working to get Rhodesian experience in the General Hospital in Umtali, he realised, from the number of war casualties being treated there, that the situation along the border was much more serious than was generally believed. On that day he came to inform me that he could no longer remain in the country, and he wished to terminate his contract. He said that the situation was much too dangerous, and, however much he regretted it, he thought that his obligation to his family came first. With this I agreed. It was proposed then that he might exchange places with another doctor, a nun of the same Order as those working in Regina Coeli, and that she might perhaps come from her hospital in the Transkei and go there to take his place.

Two days later I set off for another Mission, in Chiduku Reserve in the Rusape area, but when I arrived at the priest's house at Rusape I received an urgent message to go to Triashill Mission in the

Inyanga area to meet the priest and two European Sisters from Avila Mission. When I arrived there I heard to my great dismay that Father X had left the Mission early in the morning, bringing with him the two Sisters and all their belongings because of threats from terrorists who had come to Avila the night before.

The story, as I heard it from him, was that on the previous night, while at supper, he and Sister Vianney were summoned out into the darkness by two men who had guns at the ready. When they met they saw some other armed men lurking in the shadows some distance away. According to the priest, he and the Sister were lectured on the glories of Communism and the evils of capitalism as represented by the Kennedys, the Rockefellers and the Catholic Church. The visitors ordered the priest to reduce the school fees and the charges made at the Mission clinic. He replied that the clinic was unaided, receiving no support from the State, and that the Sisters were unpaid and the medicines had to be bought by the Mission. The terrorists told him that the Church could well afford to provide medicines freely. They then threatened that the Mission would be destroyed and other vengeance taken if their other requests for watches, radios, cameras, etc., were not granted.

After a long interview, the men went off, the priest having told them that he could not possibly meet their demands.

Naturally both he and the other members of the Mission staff were greatly frightened by the visit, and they decided that it would be unsafe for them to remain there any longer. They packed up and left early next morning, drove to Inyanga, informed the civil authorities, and without further delay arrived at

Triashill Mission, a hundred miles away from Avila, where I met them and heard their story.

The priest was very distraught and wondered if he had acted correctly in leaving the Mission and informing the authorities. I consoled him by saying that if what he told me were true, and that his night visitors were Communists who had said that they wanted to destroy the Church and its Missions, then he had acted correctly. There was a long discussion at the Mission that evening, and other missionaries joined us to decide what ought to be done, especially about Regina Coeli Mission, which was so completely isolated and so close to the Mozambique border.

It was the opinion of the majority of those discussing the matter that someone ought to go at once to Regina Coeli and find out what was happening there. I heard that the Mother Superior and one of her Sisters from Regina Coeli were at Melsetter that evening, so I phoned through and asked them to come very early in the morning, meet me at the Montclair Hotel in Inyanga where I would explain everything, and then return to their Mission in Nyamaropa. I also phoned the African priest at Mount Melleray Mission and asked him to go up as quickly as possible over the mountain to Regina Coeli to be of aid to the three European Sisters who were at the Mission.

The next day was Sunday. I celebrated Mass and preached against Communism. I met the two Franciscan Sisters at the Montclair Hotel, they having come all the way from Melsetter. I told them what had happened at Avila Mission two days earlier, and of the fears for their safety at Regina Coeli. Leading the way, I drove in my own car, with the Sisters following in theirs, up past Troutbeck

Hotel and down the escarpment to Regina Coeli Mission.

All was quiet there. The African priest had arrived, and after a short time I called together all the Sisters and the priests for a conference. I repeated what Father X had told me concerning the visitors at Avila and told the Sisters that the same might happen to them and that therefore they must consider themselves absolutely free to leave the Mission if they so wished. I told them that I could not possibly expect them to remain in such an isolated place without any protection and without even the comfort of a telephone.

Their reply was marvellous and edifying. Without any hesitation they said that they wanted to stay, that they had a duty to the patients, to the student nurses and to the Church. I informed them that the doctor and his wife would not be returning as he considered the situation too dangerous. I asked them if there was anything that I could do to make their safety more secure. They replied that they would like to have another priest at the Mission, one who could drive the car, and if possible if they could have the Land Rover that had been taken from Avila Mission. We had a very pleasant evening. All was well.

The next morning, 26th April, I drove back to Inyanga and on to Mount Melleray Mission, and from that point travelled with Father Mutume to Avila. There were many European soldiers at the priest's house. I heard from the Mission personnel that after Father X reported the terrorists at Inyanga, helicopters flew in over the mission area and army trucks full of soldiers arrived. Shooting started in the village nearby and helicopters swooped low over the fields. One African woman,

Mrs Maida Nyamapfeni, who was working in the field, ran in fright for a grass shelter nearby, and was badly wounded in the air attack. She was shot in the face, side and in both legs, but was afterwards picked up by the helicopter and flown to Bindura Hospital.

On the same day, Sunday, Mr Vinyu, on his way to Mass at the Mission, was interrogated and beaten by the Security Forces. The villagers came and reported all this at the Mission, and said that it was all Father X's fault, and that it would not have happened had he not informed. All the Mission staff were very gravely upset, so I called them, the two Sisters, the teachers, nurses, Red-Cross students and kitchen staff, and in a class room I tried to calm them, telling them that if the Sisters' safety could be guaranteed, I would try to get them to come back to the Mission. I told them that whatever Father X had done, the Security Forces themselves knew, as far back as the previous Wednesday, that terrorists had robbed a store.

I drove back that day all the way to Umtali and made arrangements to send another priest to Regina Coeli Mission as I had promised. That night the Regional Superior of the Avila Sisters, i.e. the one who is in charge of all the Sisters who are in Rhodesia, phoned from Salisbury and expressed the hope to me that whatever about Father X, 'our own two Sisters might be able to return to their Mission at Avila'. Next morning I phoned her again, asking permission to send to Avila, accompanied by two priests, one of her Sisters stationed at Mount Melleray, and to see if it would be safe for the two Sisters to go back. My diary says about this request: 'Safe from the anger of both villagers and terrorists'.

About the same time, one of my African priests came to see me, and I told him of his brother's interrogation and beating, and then, because he is a native of the Avila district, I asked him to go at once to that Mission and try to explain to the local people Father X's problem and departure from the Mission, and to endeavour to restore confidence in the missionaries. That same day also the doctor of Regina Coeli and his wife called to finalise their plans to terminate their contract of service at Regina Coeli Mission.

The news of the Avila episode travelled quickly to all parts of the country, and the very next day, 28th April, the Rhodesia Superior of the Marist Brothers, who have a large secondary school at Mount Melleray Mission, phoned me to inquire if it was safe for his community of Brothers to remain on at the Mission. The day after that I was requested by the community Sisters of Marymount College, Umtali, to meet them for a formal discussion about the closing of their College at the end of the year. It seemed that all the institutions of the Diocese were already feeling themselves threatened.

On Friday, 30th April, I received a phone call from a representative of South African newspapers asking me if it was true that I intended to withdraw all my missionaries from what he called the operational area. I replied that it was not true, and asked him – and these are the words of my diary: 'to kill the story for the safety of the Mission's Sisters'.

Shortly afterwards I had a visit from my two African priests who had come back from Avila. They asked me to do everything I could to send a European priest back there to take Father X's place, and, as they put it, to restore faith in the white missionary. I drove at once from Umtali to Avila myself, because I had to officiate at a wedding at one of the villages. I think it is useful to explain that the

Government does not recognise every ordained priest as a marriage officer, and I was the only one available to get to Avila in time.

After the wedding ceremony I drove down the road that leads from Avila to Regina Coeli Mission fairly close to the Mozambique border. I found there the Sisters of Regina Coeli very concerned, because the student nurses had organised a protest on hearing of the sudden departure of their doctor. For their nursing course to be recognised by the State it is necessary for them to be under the direction of a qualified medical doctor. Sister explained to them that in a short time one of my own priests, who is a highly qualified doctor, and who was at the time lecturing in the Royal College of Surgeons in Dublin, would be back in the country and would be available at Regina Coeli to make the nurses' course valid.

On the same day I drove to Umtali, where I found waiting for me the African Regional Superior of another Order of nuns who work at St Peter's Mission in my Diocese near Chisumbanje. This nun too, having heard of the Avila incident, was deeply concerned about the safety of the Sisters of her Order in Chisumbanje, and had come all the way from Pretoria to see for herself how things stood. I volunteered to drive her to Chisumbanje next morning. We set off the following morning, joined the convoy and went with it as far as Hot Springs. From there we proceeded to Chisumbanje, where we found everything quiet and the Sisters happy to stay on, in spite of what they had heard about Avila.

Next morning I had a phone call from the Regional Superior of the Avila Sisters telling me that her Superior General had cabled her from England saying that Father X had called on her and told her about what happened at Avila, and as a result of that she ordered that the two Avila Sisters should be sent back to Britain at once for their own safety. I told the Regional Superior to cable the Mother General in England and ask her to reconsider her decision and to inform her that I would telephone her myself as soon as I got out of the bush and away from the party line.

I returned to Umtali next day, and was delighted to hear that the two Sisters from Avila, in their anxiety to restore their good name by serving the people, had taken the risk of going back to their Mission for a quick visit. The following day I tried to phone the Superior General in England, but failed. However, subsequently, on 6th May, I did get through to her by phone and explained that it would be very bad for the reputation of the Church in Rhodesia if the Sisters were to leave the country. I even asked her to wait until I could go to Rome myself and get another opinion about the Church's reputation which would ensue were our missionaries to leave. I got in touch with the Archbishop of Salisbury, explained the situation to him and asked him to support my request that the Sisters remain on in Rhodesia.

Two days later, while in Salisbury, I was told by the Regional Superior of the Sisters that they had sent a further appeal to their Head House in England requesting permission for the Sisters to remain on in the country.

It is remarkable how, just at this time, repre-sentatives of the various religious Orders in the country suddenly expressed their concern about the future. For example, I had acted on behalf of the Rector of St George's College and the Headmis-tresses both of Nagle House, Marandellas, and of

Marymount College, Umtali, to discuss with the other Bishops what ought to be done should further deterioration in the political situation lead to the closing down of their schools. On this very day too the Superior of another Order of nuns came from Rome to visit her Sisters in Rhodesia and to find out if they were safe.

On 10th May I received another disappointment, when, from the Superior of the nuns in New York, I received a letter telling me of her Order's final decision to close down Marymount College, Umtali, at the end of the year.

On 13th May I had a meeting of my Bishop's Council, and it was agreed that I personally should go to Avila Mission and stay there alone for about a week to keep the European presence there and to allow the African priest who had been in charge to go home for a break. On that same day the Provincial Education Officer telephoned to inquire if it was true that all our teachers had left Avila Mission. I assured him that there was no truth at all in this, but I suggested that the continued presence of Security Forces on the Mission would make it a target for terrorists and would endanger the safety of the school children when they returned after the school holidays. That explains my reference to requiring the Security Forces not to remain there. The Provincial Educational Officer got in touch with the Ministry of Education and the matter was dealt with there.

On 14th May I went to Avila and took charge there for about a week. On 17th May two of the Sisters came from Mount Melleray and worked for two days at the Mission hospital. I heard from them that finally their Mother General had decided not to withdraw the Sisters permanently from Rhodesia.

On 23rd May the Regional Superior phoned to say that the two Sisters were ready to return to Avila. On 27th May I drove from Umtali to the Mission. While there I interviewed the African woman who had been wounded during the helicopter raid on 25th April. She was still receiving treatment at the Mission for her wounds. I discussed with the Mission personnel how we could best provide for the safety of the Sisters when they returned permanently.

On 1st June an incident took place which, in the light of events, proved important. A young European girl had disappeared from her home in Umtali into Mozambique and caused great concern to her parents, who were my parishioners. Her father came to my house that evening with the senior officer of the CID, and we discussed how I perhaps might act as intermediary in getting the child back to Rhodesia. In the course of the long conversation, the CID officer told me that the Church had failed in Avila by not maintaining a European presence there. The priest who had informed on the terrorists should not have run away, he said, but should have stayed on. He added: "That is just what the Communists want – Europeans to clear out so that they can take over."

I explained that I had gone back to the Mission myself to show the flag, as it were, and that the European Sisters were themselves anxious to return permanently so that the *status quo ante* should be restored. I told him of all my efforts with the Mother Superior General in England, and reminded him that if he liked to check up on me, my telephone calls would have been recorded as proof of what I had done.

Next day I was informed of the two Avila Sisters,

who were already on their way back and had arrived at Mount Melleray Mission. I drove there next morning with supplies and brought the two Sisters back to the Mission which they had left with Father X on 24th April. We received a wonderful welcome from all of the villagers, but especially from the hospital staff.

To show the character of Sister Vianney and her willingness to serve in spite of danger, I would like to tell you that on the very next morning, 5th June, she received a sick call asking her to go out to a distant village to assist a woman who had already been a full day in labour. The only motor car available at the Mission was my little Volkswagen, which was quite useless for the purpose. Straight away Sister solved the problem by getting a driver for the Mission tractor and trailer and set off with it into the bundu. Hours later she returned on the tractor with the baby safely delivered and the mother well.

I go on following my diary to 20th June, when in Umtali I met the Superior General of the nuns who work at Regina Coeli hospital. She had come all the way from Ireland to visit the convents of her Order in Ethiopia, Kenya, Zambia and South Africa, but her great concern was for the safety of those at Regina Coeli. Fortunately she had gone there, spent some days with the nuns, and was returning to Ireland confident that they could remain there in safety.

On 26th June the Regional Superior of the Avila Sisters wished to visit the Mission and see for herself how the nuns were settling in before leaving for England to report to the Superior General. I brought her there where she remained until the following day. I then drove her back to another convent of her Sisters near Headlands. During the time of my visit to the Mission I heard that terrorists were in the vicinity and I did not report their presence for the reasons which I will soon explain to the court.

THE WHY

Before I endeavour to explain to the court my reasons for acting as I did, permit me to outline some of the principles which influenced my decision. I accept, first of all, that obedience to legal authority is a moral duty. However, if the State demands obedience against the antecedent duty of fulfilling one's existential ends, then obedience becomes evil.

Again I must ask the court to bear in mind that the Church, and churchmen such as I, are conscious of the strong distinction between morality and law. They regard human rights and their correlative duties as a manifestation in human nature of God's eternal law, and in consequence they hold that they are anterior to society, to any arbitrary contract, majority principle, public opinion or poll. Into this category, and I mention those only which are pertinent to the present issue, fall such rights as the right to life, to bodily integrity and well-being, the right to a good reputation, to an honest representation, the right to act in accordance with the right norms of one's conscience, the right to worship God, to practise one's religion, both in public and in private, and to enjoy religious liberty. Man has the imprescriptible right also to be correctly informed about public events, and, as if to crown it all, he has the right to have all his rights – I have, as I say, only mentioned a few of them – safeguarded by law. Finally, he has a right to a protection that is impartial, effective and inspired by true justice.

Man perceives and acknowledges the imperative

of the divine law through the mediation of conscience, properly informed. The protection and promotion in an effective manner of such freedoms ranks among the essential duties of Government.

Another matter of great importance in my case is that, as a Bishop of the Church, I have a particular obligation to build up and to preserve what Christian teaching calls the Kingdom of God on earth. The whole reason for my office is that I should dedicate myself completely to the work of advancing the Christian religion. Should this task of penetrating and perfecting the temporal sphere of things with the spirit of the Gospel of Jesus Christ conflict with my obligation of obedience to the civil authority, I know at once where my duty lies. No matter what the consequences may be for myself personally, should it even involve my life, I must always put what I regard as the good of the Church before my own personal convenience, even before what the State commands. In other words, I must obey God rather than men.

This does not mean that between Church and State there need necessarily be any conflict. The political community exists for the common good, and so it follows that the Church regards as worthy of praise and consideration the work of all those who, as a service to others, dedicate themselves to the welfare of the State and undertake the burdens of the task.

But, and this is vital in my consideration, political authority, whether in the community as such or in institutions represented by the State, must always be exercised within the limits of morality and on behalf of a dynamically conceived common good, according to a juridical order enjoying legal status. When such is the case, citizens are conscience-bound to obey. This fact, which I here acknowledge clearly, reveals the responsibility, dignity and importance of those who govern.

Two phrases just used call for comment, for example, 'enjoying legal status' and 'conscience-bound'. Although the community of nations disputes the claim, the Government of Rhodesia believes that it enjoys legal status. I am here in court at this moment for this reason. I have no alternative.

That is not quite correct. I could have refused to attend the court voluntarily, and might instead have been brought here by force. Alternatively, having my passport still in my possession, I might have fled the country, putting myself beyond the jurisdiction of this court.

However, I am still here, first of all because I believe that I have been, by divine providence, appointed to promote God's work in the Diocese of Umtali, and here is where my duty lies, hence here I must remain. Secondly, even in the court I welcome the opportunity of explaining my behaviour and of giving concrete witness to the concern of the Church for social justice. Finally I am here because, however unpleasant my situation, both to me and to my people, I recognise that there has to be some legal authority. The alternative is anarchy.

I am not an anarchist. Through all the thirty years I have lived in Rhodesia and worked for the welfare of all its people, I have counselled the use of constitutional means for obtaining redress of grievances, grievances affecting the vast majority of the population. Such grievances, based on a racist ethic, denied them equality under the law, equal admittance to the economic, cultural, social and political life of the country, and a fair share in the nation's wealth, and left power, responsibility and decision making in the hands of a race segment of the people.

Moreover, I would like to insist on this, my criticisms of the civil administration have not been confined to the present Government. Long before the Rhodesia Front Party was even heard of, I was exercising my duty as a citizen by openly and lawfully pointing out certain evils in the State in an effort to obtain redress of grievances, and ultimately that peace which it is greatly the work of churchmen to promote.

Never once have I advocated the use of violence. Instead I have consistently acted in the belief that the two classic non-violent means of protest were the only means justifiable, that is, the mobilisation of public opinion and an appeal to a superior forum of justice.

These methods have been tried and have failed. Instead of hearing the joint appeals of the Christian leaders in this country, the Government has refused to do anything really significant to change the unjust social structures which call down on us the condemnation of the free world. Even at this crucial moment of our history, the really vital proposals of the Quénet Report have been rejected. And the electorate, anaesthetised by state-controlled radio and television, remains unmoved.

Neither did an appeal to a superior forum of justice make any difference. The authoritative report on *Racial Discrimination and Repression in Southern Rhodesia,* a legal study prepared by the International Commission of Jurists and published in March of this year, 1976, might as well never have been written as far as those who rule Rhodesia are concerned.

It was the same most recently with my Open Letter to the Government.

This being so, and since all other legitimate means of redress of serious violations of human rights have been tried without success, surely it is not only permissible but even an obligation that forms of passive resistance should be exercised in defence of the human condition against the intransigent oppression of the State?

Both politically and morally, passive resistance I look upon, as indeed the Church looks upon it, as the only proper means of protecting the liberties of citizens, when, as I believe in this case, the Government abuses its powers.

It is clear from what I have already said that I cannot and never did in conscience approve of the racist ideology, which I see at the basis of life in Rhodesia today. Equally it should be clear that I have never, in the course of all my years here, seemed by my silence to connive at the unjust situation. I could not. The teaching of the Church utterly condemns racial discrimination as contrary to the natural dignity of the human person and to the brotherhood of men. There has never been any doubt in my mind about the matter. Christianity and any teaching of racial discrimination are mutually exclusive.

Addressing the United Nations on apartheid in 1974, Pope Paul stated: "Men rightly consider unjustifiable and reject as inadmissible the tendency to maintain or introduce legislation or behaviour systematically inspired by racialist prejudice," and he added: "As long as the rights of all the peoples, among them the right to self-determination and independence, are not duly recognised and honoured, there cannot be true and lasting peace, even though the abusive power of arms may for a time prevail over the reactions of those opposed. For as long as, within individual natural communities, those in power do not nobly respect the rights and legitimate freedoms of the citizens, tranquility and order, even though they can be maintained by force, remain nothing but a deceptive and insecure sham no longer worthy of a society of civilised men."

These words of Pope Paul are directed to men of all faiths and of none, but in the Rhodesian situation they appear to have a pointed validity, and I have accepted them as a directive for pastoral action. To professing Christians, however, the Pontiff gave more specific reasons for denouncing racial injustices when he added: "The message which we offer – and it is at the same time advice, counsel and injunction for Christian consciences – to every group or state or nation, is what we have learned from Him, whom we represent (meaning Christ): You are all brothers."

I pay particular attention to this argument in order to show that I could not possibly, as an ordinary human being concerned with social justice, much less as a Christian, and never under any circumstances as a Bishop, encourage or support by my silence any regime which grossly and blatantly promotes legislation and behaviour systematically inspired by racialist prejudice, and as a consequence so utterly opposed to the teaching of Christ. To permit myself, or those working under my jurisdiction, to appear to collaborate with such an unjust and unchristian system for the sake of avoiding the penalties of the law, even death or imprisonment, would destroy not only our credibility as Christians, but would cause irreparable damage to the Christian message among all thinking people, especially among the African population of this country at this time.

Were this to happen, Christian missionaries might as well withdraw from the country, because the people would reject them as deceivers: men and women who preached one thing but practised another. The chances of Christianity, even in its Government-sponsored, controlled and emasculated form, being tolerated here in time to come, would, by such connivance, appear minimal.

And this, I hope, illustrates one aspect of the dilemma which not only I have to face, but all my missionaries, and, indeed, everyone who takes his Christian faith seriously in this country today. To support racial discrimination, either directly by practising it oneself, or by aiding those institutions based on it, and at the same time to claim to be a Christian, is to bring Christianity into disrepute and – this is important in the context of Southern Africa at this time – to leave the way open for Communism.

From 21st April until the end of June I had travelled from one end of the Diocese to the other with the Superiors of the different orders of nuns who had come all the way from Europe to see for themselves whether it would be safe for their Sisters to continue working here. You will remember too how strenuously I worked to persuade them that the Sisters should be permitted to remain; how I also told the Superior of the Marist Brothers that his subjects too should stay and continue their work for the Diocese. At the same time I received from the Mother Superior of another Order, the Marymount Sisters, official intimation that they would have to close the College in Umtali at the end of the year. The Junior School at the Dominican Convent in Umtali was also due to close for good at the end of this year, and now I was faced with the very real problem of having to close down all our other Church institutions in the African areas, if, by reporting the presence of terrorists, these institutions would have to close and the missionaries leave Rhodesia.

A senior officer of the CID exhorted me to keep all the Missions going and not give terrorists the impression that they were in control of the country.

Another important aspect of the problem lies in this, that the dilemma I was placed in would not be confined to me, or to my Diocese, or to any one Christian denomination. It would soon become commonplace, as the infiltrations of terrorists increased and the intransigent attitude of the Government made the local people more ready to receive them as liberators.

I have already pointed out some of the benefits which accrue to Rhodesia by the presence of missionaries. In particular I showed what a small unit, such as the Diocese of Umtali, with its educational and health services, has done to develop the country and benefit all sections of the community. Were we and all other Christian missionaries to be forced to close down all these institutions by being compelled to violate conscience and obey the laws of men rather than those of God, Rhodesia would very greatly suffer.

One may well ask, is this what the Government wants? Is this what the legislation we are dealing with envisages? I might well ask myself also which is better, to keep my Missions in existence and my missionaries in the field for the general good of Rhodesia, a good which can be equated with the good of the Christian Church, or must I, in blind obedience, obey a particular ordinance of men and so bring the whole work of Christianity to an end?

What does the Government want? Obedience to its laws about reporting the presence of its enemies, which it probably knows about anyway, or the continuing presence of the Christian Churches and the consequent benefit to Rhodesia now and in the years to come?

I certainly know where my duty lies. It lies in preserving the good name and consequently the continued presence of the Church in Rhodesia, no matter what the laws of men demand. I cannot be false to conscience. The law cannot compel me.

In my belief that passive resistance is permissible when other means of protest have failed, I would like to remind the court that in the case we are dealing with there was no kind of exceptional contribution made by me or by any of my missionaries enabling the enemies of the State to continue their campaign of rebellion. There was no question of our providing the weapons of war or the financial means of obtaining such military equipment. In this respect we are pacifist. Simple medical aid was all that was permitted and given, and that in virtue of the Christian imperative of charity. Could anything be more consonant with a non-violent approach to the problem, more in conformity with the practice of passive resistance?

On the very problem presented to missionaries when they are confronted with requests from the enemies of the State for medical aid, or even food and clothing—anything, in fact, apart from the arms of war—may I attempt to describe in some detail the very situation at Avila Mission when a letter asking for medical help was handed in to the Mission hospital on behalf of terrorists.

The Church staff consisted of two African Sisters, two European Sisters, both State Registered Nurses, and two priests, one a European and the other an African. They live in a very isolated part of the country, as the map shows. They are at least ten miles away from the nearest telephone, and that has only been introduced fairly recently, I believe, into a new police camp. The road leading to the Mission is hazardous at all times of the year. Their nearest European neighbours are at another Mission, twelve miles south of them. There cannot be, in normal times, more than fifteen Europeans in the whole area, which is contiguous with Mozambique, and in most difficult terrain.

What is anyone, missionary or lay person, African or European, to do when approached for medical help in such circumstances? To deny such help in peacetime, or to inquire into the religious or political beliefs of the needy person before giving aid, is quite contrary to the Christian conscience, as it is to the high principles of the profession of medicine.

In these conditions, particularly the conditions of a guerrilla war, when the guerrillas, heavily armed, come to lonely outposts where there is neither the protection of weapons and ammunition or even the comfort and relative protection of a telephone, what can anyone do but obey demands made under threats, expressed or implied, of violent retaliation?

Government progaganda has, as I said, given gruesome details of the mutilation alleged to have been carried out by terrorists on those who have dared to inform on them. We have been told that such informers have had their lips and ears hacked off, and even worse.

What is the unfortunate missionary, defenceless and isolated, expected to do under the circumstances? Inform and be mutilated or murdered sooner or later, when the Security Forces have been and gone and the missionary is quite alone again?

What does the State expect? Heroic resistance, superhuman courage, martyrdom, to maintain a system which compounds social injustices and supports the privileged conditions of the few, a system condemned by the civilised world? What does the State demand of this young nun who has given up home and family and who has dedicated herself for life under the vows of poverty, chastity and obedience to the service of the underprivileged, the hungry, the thirsty, the naked, the stranger, the prisoner – in whom Christ himself says He is to be found, in whom He is to be seen and served?

Does the State believe that it can so compel the conscience as to make such a person as Sister Vianney, or, indeed, any other Christian, deny her faith and renounce her duty and be disloyal to the Church she belongs to? Does the Government of Rhodesia insist, for the preservation of its own narrow needs, that we must serve men rather than God?

Is not this precisely a violation of the basic human right to freedom of conscience, freedom to worship God according to the right norm of conscience, freedom to practise religion both in public and in private?

I keep in mind that the service of the sick and the needy, in the name of God, is every bit an act of religion as is public or private worship.

Nor is this all. Has not the person in the circumstances described, threatened on the one hand by the penalties of the law and on the other by the extreme and immediate danger of death or mutilation – has not such a person the fundamental right to life? To compel anyone, like this young nun, to endanger herself, or to sacrifice her life for the maintenance of an unjust social system, is surely more than any civilised, legal authority can demand. Does the order to report in such circumstances not, in principle at least, mean a violation of the citizen's right to life itself? Is this not another human right lightly violated?

Does this court believe that the State can compel anyone to give his life, or risk it recklessly, for the observance of its laws? I do not think so; though, indeed, in these days, anything can happen. This, however, I can say: I, as a Bishop of a Diocese, cannot, by any authority which I possess, and would not, were it within my power, compel any subject of mine to risk life or mutilation under any circumstances whatsoever, least of all in the circumstances we are dealing with, when to obey the law of this land would bring discredit to the Church. In fact, during the days of the Avila incident, I went myself to the Mission rather than insist that another should put himself in danger.

And this brings me to another aspect of the right to life and its relevance to the present issue. By informing, not only does the informer prejudice his own safety, but he deliberately endangers the lives of others. The moment the Security Forces hear of the presence of terrorists, they at once embark on their mission of extermination. All that is required of them is, as the law (Indemnity and Compensation Act 1976) itself declares, that they should act in good faith. The terrorists themselves, of course, are the first victims to be sought out and mercilessly annihilated.

What of the informer? Is he or she not responsible for the deaths of such persons? What of the missionary, who knows more intimately than anyone else the daily sufferings of the African people, their near despair, as they see the State make little effort to treat them as full citizens in their own country? Is the missionary-informer not responsible for the death of any young man or woman who, in defence of his own fundamental rights, takes up arms for what he believes is a just cause?

But what about the other people who become the victims of the informer's co-operation? I refer, of course, to the villagers in the area where the terrorists are known to have been. Rhodesia knows what their fate is likely to be. Certainly the missionaries and the African people know. Once the informer speaks, the unfortunate villagers can themselves expect to come under attack from the Security Forces, as indeed happened at Avila the day after the presence of the terrorists was revealed.

First come the helicopters, sweeping low and firing at anything black and bifurcated moving suspiciously in the village or the bush nearby. Then come the troops, armed to the teeth with all their modern weaponry. Then others with trained and fierce dogs, and the comfort of the law to encourage everybody. In their determination to seek out and destroy their enemies, they know that they can carry on regardless, there are no holds barred.

The former Minister of Defence has given them a clear directive granting them unlimited freedom of action. Speaking in the House of Assembly on 2nd July of 1976, the Minister declared: "If villagers harbour terrorists, and terrorists are found running about in the villages, naturally they will be bombed and destroyed in any manner which the commander on the spot considers desirable in the suitable prosecution of a successful campaign." He added: "My first concern is to eradicate the terrorists, and civilians mixed up with them have only themselves to blame."

Shocked by such remarks, I wrote a letter published in *The Rhodesia Herald* on 10th July, 1976, where I said: 'It is necessary to remind the Government, and the Minister of Defence in particular, that political authority must always be exercised within the limits of morality. The successful prosecution of a war cannot justify the indiscriminate killing of people. Such a wicked and cowardly preparedness to bomb whole villages and perhaps kill innocent people, children particularly, who would have had no responsible contacts with terrorists, is wholly reprehensible and unpardonable in a Minister of the Government.'

I was, of course, at once attacked in the Press and misrepresented. But what I insist on here is another of the effects of informing. When the local people in their villages become the immediate target for the indiscriminate attacks of the Security Forces, if the Christian missionary is the informer, the whole local community understandably blame him. And they blame not only him but the whole organisation to which he belongs. Not only his Church gets the blame, but Christianity itself is condemned as a fraud, as the agent of oppression, and is accused of teaching the brotherhood of all men in creation and in redemption, and of contradicting it in practice – even becoming the willing accomplice in the bombing and destroying of villages and in the killing of innocent women and children.

This is fact. The village next to Avila was attacked. I myself recorded the details of the terrifying event from a young African woman who was machine-gunned from a helicopter. Her hospital charts from Bindura, Inyanga and Avila hospitals are in the keeping of the Justice and Peace

Commission of which I am President.

Apart from my inability and unwillingness to command my missionaries to report and so imperil their own lives, the lives of the local people are endangered, and in consequence harm is done to the good name of the Christian Church. I believe that, as the Church's responsible authority, I have the prior and more compelling obligation of doing all in my power to protect the lives of my people than to protect the lives of the Security Forces.

It is an accepted principle in the Christian Church that the Bishop must act as the shepherd of the flock, the pastor of his people. It is his duty, as a spiritual Father, so to protect all who look to him for leadership that, if it should be necessary, he should not hesitate to shield them from danger. He should be prepared to give his life for his people, especially if their actions, performed in the service of the Church, should put them in danger.

With that ideal before me, I told my missionaries that I would hold myself entirely responsible for their actions, both in giving medicines to the terrorists and in not reporting their presence. In doing so, I am convinced, not only that I was acting correctly as their Bishop, but that I was actually fulfilling a further obligation, namely of taking more care of the defenceless missionaries than of the armed forces, who, I presumed, were well able and well equipped to defend themselves. In short, I believe my greater duty, from every point of view, lay in protecting the lives of innocent and defenceless people than in protecting soldiers.

There is even more to it. Those of us who live close to the African people in these difficult days and who enjoy their confidence know how difficult it is to identify strangers who come into the villages, and indeed how unreliable their messages can sometimes be, and even for what purpose they issue commands.

It is widely believed, and I think the State will readily admit it, that African members of the Security Forces have been infiltrated among the terrorists and masquerade in their guise.

The danger of reporting terrorists who deliberately make their presence known is that the terrorists might be laying a trap for the Security Forces. If this succeeds, the African missionary may be accused of being a party to the trap.

I come now to an aspect of the problem which concerns anyone who, like myself, belongs to the clerical profession. It is a generally accepted principle, in Western society at least, that the State recognises and respects the confidence which the laity of all denominations place in their clergy. As a Catholic Bishop may I make it at once quite clear that I am not here speaking of that peculiar quality of confidence which, in our Church, is given to a priest under the seal of the Confessional. That is a special matter altogether and need not be discussed here. It does not concern us.

What I am concerned with, however, is the widely acknowledged immunity which the custom of Western nations allows to the confidences which a citizen places in a minister of religion. I believe that the basis for this immunity lies in the recognition by the State of its subsidiary function in human affairs, and its acknowledgement of the supremacy of the moral order, in which the sacred relationship between man and his God is given primacy.

The Christian clergyman, in terms of his very function, must appear to men as offering to them the mercy and reconciliation of his God. No one, even the greatest criminal, the most debased, the most hardened sinner, may ever be refused his counsel or his word of mercy. He must be prepared to understand the frailty of human nature, man's tendency to evil, the almost overpowering compulsion of temptation.

What a loss to society if such a source of good were to be set aside. After all, it is the *ought*, the power of conscience, the sense of religion, not physical necessity, which determines man's actions and which can reform society itself by inculcating obedience to the Creator's laws. By such willing obedience men may even be brought to achieve, in their daily lives, something of that order and peace which is manifest through physical necessity in the rest of creation.

Take the case in question, the Avila incident. Were anyone, even a terrorist, to approach me for food or clothing or medicine, I would certainly not refuse him, if it were at all possible for me to give him ordinary help. Neither would I place his life in danger by informing on him. If such a one were to come to me for counsel, I would deal with him in the same manner and would consider myself bound in conscience to remind him of God's command 'Thou shalt not kill', and try to persuade him to use nonviolent means of seeking redress of his grievances. All of which sounds very well, and presumes the man to be well-disposed and docile. Were he otherwise, were he to threaten me with death or mutilation or anything similar, I suppose I would be as cowardly as any other ordinary person in the same circumstances.

But there is another possible variation in the case. Suppose, for instance, I am conducting a religious service, and I notice, or have brought to my attention by others, an enemy of the State among the congregation of worshippers. Am I supposed to report his presence to the Security Forces, and so make his act of worship the occasion of capture or death? Is obedience to the State to be regarded as a greater good to be sought and obtained than an individual's act of acknowledging the worship he owes to his God? Am I, the minister of religion, to play the turncoat and become the servant of the State rather than the servant of God? In other words, am I bound to obey men rather than God?

I cannot see that as a Christian, and certainly as a Bishop, I will be performing a service to my God or to His Church, or even to civil society itself, if I be compelled by law to make my ministry in this manner a servant of the State, no longer a ministry of mercy or reconciliation, but rather an instrument of vengeance. Rather, I choose what I conceive to be the greater good, and with a clear and informed conscience accept what penalty the law may provide for my disobedience. I do not despise the law. I simply obey a higher law. I must obey God rather than men. I cannot do both simultaneously in these circumstances.

It seems, therefore, that in demanding that I obey its laws and inform about the presence of its enemies, the State of Rhodesia, as at present constituted, and with its present unwillingness to modify its policies, places an intolerable burdern, not only on me as a Catholic Bishop, but, in fact, on every other Christian worthy of the name. It is asking what is morally impossible. It is coercing conscience. *Ad impossile nemo tenetur*. No one is bound to perform the impossible.

In stating this ancient legal truth, one is reminded of another problem. Let me put it this way: Can the State, under the threat of death or of any other serious punishment, such as would be a long period of imprisonment, compel a citizen to perform an act which is not absolutely, but only relatively necessary to the common weal? This is the situation, I believe, in many instances where people are expected to report the presence of terrorists. In fact in many cases the Security Forces are already aware that terrorists are around. They obtain this information as a result of their own activities, and they also get it from the hundreds of paid informers, people who are prepared to play the traitor, very often simply to revenge themselves on their own personal enemies.

Take the Avila incident, for example. The very day I arrived at the Mission and was informed of the note handed in on behalf of the terrorists asking for medicines – on that very afternoon Security Forces visited the Mission and informed the priest there that terrorists were in the neighbourhood and had the previous day robbed a store and a bus. Is not any additional reporting by a missionary or anyone else in such a case a work of supererogation? Is one to be severely punished for not performing such a duty? In any well-ordered political community where authority is solidly based on the consent of the governed, such unnecessary legislation should not obtrude itself on our notice.

Closely connected with this argument is the fact that the Security Forces are not really in control of the situation anywhere in the operational area of Rhodesia. I say this in spite of all the State propaganda to the contrary.

Missionaries of all denominations are in a far better position to know what is, in fact, taking place than the Government is. They are widely placed all over the country; they live close to the people; they know them intimately and enjoy their confidence.

They are with their people all the time, and not like the members of the Security Forces, here one day and gone the next. Scarcely a thing happens in the Tribal Trust Lands that does not come quickly to the notice of the missionaries. Theirs is a closely knit organisation, and the news of the happenings in one area quickly travels to another.

It is simple fact that the general public in Rhodesia, certainly the European population, knows only a fraction of the activities of the nationalists everywhere throughout the country. All the Security Forces are able to do is to move into an area where terrorists are reported to have appeared, carry out punitive raids, stay on for a little while and then move on to another disturbed area to do the same.

Moreover, the strength of the African people's opposition to the present Government is daily on the increase. Time and numbers are on their side, and they know it. No matter what the State propaganda may declare, the African people already sense that the Security Forces are no longer in control of events.

The practice of informing is, as far as the successful prosecution of the war goes, quite useless. The Security Forces generally manage to kill only innocent villagers in retaliation for the presence of the guerrillas. Moreover, by such action they not only further antagonise the African people, but they promote the cause of those whom they seek to eliminate.

I have pleaded guilty to the charges preferred against me, and welcome this opportunity of explaining to the court the reasons for my actions. I believe that I had no alternative but to act as I did. The good reputation of the Church had, in my opinion, to be preserved at all costs. The lives of local villagers, innocent and unarmed, had also to be protected, as had – and in this case as their Bishop I had a very compelling responsibility – the lives of my missionary personnel. The cumulative effect of these arguments convinced me at the time, and is even more coercive now, that I have no alternative but to break the law. In doing so, I believe that I was not in any way acting as an anarchist. I believe that, since neither I nor any of my missionaries made any positive contribution to the promoting of violence through providing arms or ammunition, my actions can reasonably be regarded as legitimate acts of passive resistance – nothing more.

It is most important that a solution to this problem be found as soon as possible. The incident which took place at Avila is not an isolated one, as is well known to the authorities. It is repeated frequently in different forms. The common good is bound to suffer if, throughout the country, the problem is left unsolved, and if members of the medical profession, churchmen and others in allied occupations, do not know how they are to reconcile the commands of conscience with those of the civil authority.

While I was still struggling to keep all our missionary activity alive and to preserve the medical and educational services they provide for the country, the general situation continued to deteriorate. Outside pressures on Rhodesia increased, yet within the country itself the authorities continued in their determination to resist meaningful change of the unhappy social structures. The hopes once placed in the Quénet Report on Racial Discrimination were dashed and seen to have been illusory. Meanwhile, from every corner of the country, through the information that missionaries possessed, came increasing evidence of further infiltration by members of the nationalist movement, and a growing realisation that the masses of the African people were welcoming them and affording them every support.

On the morning of August 11th, Umtali came under mortar and rocket attack from Mozambique. On that very morning too I received news of the arrest and detention without charge of one of my African priests. Even at that late hour I decided that I would make a further appeal to the Government by sending to the Prime Minister and to each member of his Cabinet an open letter pleading for an immediate change in what I called 'its present tragic course of action'. I indicated quite clearly the increasing difficulty that Church leaders were having in reconciling their Christian principles with the demands made on them by racist legislation. The very problem of medical or other non-military aid to the enemies of the State was discreetly indicated in my letter to let the authorities know that it was an urgent and widespread one. A mission doctor was at that time still awaiting trial for a somewhat similar offence.

In my Open Letter I put it this way to the members of the Cabinet: 'Over the years, and as a matter of principle, the Catholic Church has had to refuse to practise racial segregation in its schools and hospitals, or to limit to the percentage laid down by your administration the service of Christian charity which is commanded of it by the Gospel. Today an equally important decision will have to be taken whenever or wherever the charity of the Church is sought by those who are in conscience opposed to your regime. Have not those who honestly believe that they fight for the basic human rights of the people a justifiable claim on the Church for the spiritual administration of the clergy? How can one counsel loyalty and obedience to your ordinances when to do so is tantamount to giving approval to the manifold injustices you inflict? To keep silence about one reign of oppression in order the better to combat what you alone consider to be another, is wholly unacceptable'.

And then I ended by saying: 'If intensification of racial hatred, widespread urban guerilla activity, increased destruction of property and fearful loss of life are to be avoided, if the whole sub-continent of Africa is not to be engulfed in a cruel war, you must without delay change your present course of action'.

Notice I did not attempt – because it is not within my competency – to give any specific solutions. That is for men of state, not for me. All I begged for – and I think this is the right of any citizen, as it is his duty to point out defects if he sees that anything is wrong – all I begged for was that the Government should, without delay, change its present course of action. My final words were: 'It is up to you to give the lead. The fate of Rhodesia and its people is in your hands'.

And what did Government do about my appeal? Some will say that it filed these charges against me. The State has officially denied this. At least one Minister commented not too politely on my Open Letter in the House of Assembly. But even now nothing really worthwhile has been done, and people like me, who work for the welfare of Rhodesia, are regarded as its enemies.

What a frightful comment on our society. As I said in the beginning of this statement, I am concerned in this problem at its local and at its international level with the human person; with the need for the recognition in law and in fact of his unique identity, with his fundamental dignity, with his unprescriptible rights as a purpose-made creature of the Almighty with his rights and duties as a member of society.

This has been the leitmotiv of this whole unsworn statement of mine. Think of it in this way: The whole civilised world is appalled and reacts with horror, humiliation and hurt when a mentally deranged person attacks and tries to mutilate a great work of artistic genius, such as the Pietà of Michelangelo, and yet he can remain unmoved and unconcerned when God's own handiwork, that is the human person himself, is attacked in his very essence, in his basic rights and is mutilated and treated as non-man by his fellows who claim to be sane and civilised. Is this not the tragedy and horror of the racist state?

However, I am glad to be here today to bear witness to the practical concern of the Church that God's will, manifested in social justice, be done in Rhodesia. I am grateful to you, your worship and gentlemen, and to your associates, for your quite exceptional patience. I thank for their testimony to the truth all those who have given evidence.

Throughout the weeks that have passed since I was first indicted, I have been greatly comforted by the words which the first Bishop of Rome, Peter the Fisherman, addressed to those who might, in the centuries to come, have to appear before magistrates to answer for their adherence to the faith which they were given. He said: "No one can hurt you if you are determined to do only what is right. If you do have to suffer for being good, you will count it a blessing. There is no need to be afraid or to worry about them. Simply reverence the Lord Christ in your hearts, and always have your answer ready for people who ask you the reason for the hope that you all have. But give it with courtesy and respect and with a clear conscience, so that those who slander you when you are living a good life in Christ may be proved wrong in the accusations that they bring. And if it is the will of God that you should suffer, it is better to suffer for doing right than for doing wrong."

I. The Judgement

II. An Independent Report

I. THE JUDGEMENT

What follows is the main part of the judgement of the High Court of Rhodesia by Chief Justice MacDonald. The technicalities of Bishop Lamont's appeal have been omitted.

The appellant's statement contained many expressions of opinion of a political nature which are inextricably interwoven with the purely factual and legal aspects of this case. These political views are introduced in mitigation of his offences, and it is not possible for this Court to avoid dealing with them in assessing the weight of the plea in mitigation.

The appellant in his statement acknowledges that as a priest he must not concern himself with politics. He says: "The priest normally should not involve himself in ideological and partisan disputes, since this would jeopardise his function as a mediator and would possibly tarnish the purity of his message and indeed his freedom as a representative of the Church."

He acknowledges that there must be some legal authority and that obedience to legal authority is a moral duty. In conformity with his view that a priest should not involve himself in politics, the appellant says that it is not within his 'competence to give specific solutions' and adds 'that is for men of state, not for me'.

For obvious reasons the Church may not make itself responsible for the political structures of a country. If it were to do so, it would immediately assume a political role and, to use a favourite word of the appellant, would lose 'credibility' as a church. But just as a church may not accept the responsibility for creating political structures, so too, for precisely the same reason, it cannot accept the responsibility of destroying them. Indeed, the arguments against a destructive role in politics are even more compelling than the argument against a creative role.

Wholly inexcusably and quite inconsistently, the appellant throughout his statement indicates in the clearest terms that he is prepared to accept the role of a political activist in 'dismantling unjust social structures. . . .' The following passages reveal the appellant's political activities:

'The official document published at the end of the Synod and entitled *Justice in the World* clearly stated the obligation imposed by conscience and by the Christian faith on all who professed that faith to take positive action to promote justice in the world and to work through peaceful means *for the dismantling of those unjust structures which denied other human beings integral human development.*'

'This ought to explain much of my activity here in Rhodesia *in my work for the promotion of a sane order and the eradication of injustices in any shape or form.*'

'I cannot too greatly emphasise the need for the Church to be seen here and now as a courageous voice in the denunciation of injustice, particularly those felt by the African people, and *as a committed and active agent in the peaceful dismantling of unjust social structures wherever they exist.*'

'*I believe that if this system of government be*

permitted to continue without any change what-soever, without any attempt at providing equality under the law and equal opportunity for all men, then the danger of another Nuremberg could be very real indeed.'

'. . . anyone who wants peace here, must surely recognise that *the laws* which have built up and continue to maintain such national disorder *must quickly be revoked* by the rulers; *the unjust social structures must, without delay, be dismantled.* In short, institutional violence must be abolished if racial war, with the most horrible consequences, is to be avoided.'

'Instead of hearing the joint appeal of the Christian leaders of this country, the Government refused to do anything really significant *to change the unjust social structure,* which calls down on us the condemnation of the free world.'

'This being so and since all other legitimate means of redress of serious violations of human rights have been tried without success, *surely it is not only permissible but even an obligation that forms of passive resistance should be exercised in defence of the human condition against the intransigent oppression of the State.*

Both politically and morally, passive resistance I look upon, as indeed the Church looks upon it, *as the only proper means of protecting the liberties of citizens,* when, as I believe in this case, the Government abuses its powers.'

What the appellant is saying in the clearest terms is that he is prepared to work actively to 'dismantle social structures'. Moreover, he is prepared to take active steps to bring about these changes without first satisfying one of the criteria which the appellant says must be fulfilled before revolutionary activity is permissible, namely that 'there be a reasonable prospect of success and of the setting up of an objectively better government'. Since the appellant has expressed the view that the terrorists will win, and since the evidence is overwhelming that the terrorists are members of a Communist organisation, how is he able to satisfy himself that his support for the terrorists would result in 'an objectively better government'.

In the course of his statement the appellant on more than one occasion makes the generalisation that Africans in Rhodesia have been oppressed by European rule.

Missionaries work almost exclusively in the African field, more often than not in remote areas of the country. Some serve for a short period only in Rhodesia and then move on to another country or return to their country of origin. Others devote a lifetime in the secular and religious service of the Africans in this country. It is understandable, in these circumstances, that missionaries tend to identify themselves with African causes and aspirations and to see the problems of the country through the eyes of the African with whom they work closely at all times, in much the same way as Europeans, living in a wholly European environment, tend to see the problems through European eyes. Neither, in the result, achieves a wholly balanced view and the realisation that both sections of the community are completely interdependent and complementary to each other.

In assessing the moral guilt of the appellant, it is important not to lose sight of these tendencies. Unhappily, some missionaries appear to have a preconceived idea that their mission in life, in part at least, will be to save and deliver the African from what he or she has been led to believe is the exploitation by and rapacity of the European. The truth is that each section of the community is heavily in debt to the other; the European to the African for providing, in the formative years of Rhodesia, the sinew and muscle of all that has been achieved in so short a time, the African to the European for establishing law and order, without which nothing, least of all missionary work, could prosper and for introducing much-needed skills and expertise. It serves no good purpose and leads only to acrimony to attempt to make a comparative assessment of the contribution made by each section of the community. Such an attempt will always prove to be a sterile exercise because the truth is simply that the changes which have been brought about, transforming Rhodesia from a primitive country, racked by tribal division and conflict and plagued by barbaric practices of witchcraft, to a country with a highly sophisticated twentieth century economy with a higher average standard of living for both African and European than almost any other African country, could not have been achieved by either section of the community without the other.

The problems which now exist are not the bitter fruit of a colonial experiment which has failed, but, on the contrary, stem directly from the success of that experiment in creating the peaceful climate in which there has been a burgeoning, not only of commerce and industry, but also of the potential of all its inhabitants. Within the lifetime of a single person, this country has witnessed a very substantial number of the African section of the community moving swiftly from a wholly rural and primitive existence to participate in a modern Western society and from a pagan and barbaric society to a substantially Christian society. So swift has been this transformation that the institutions created by the Europeans when Rhodesia was established have not fully adapted themselves to it and it is understandable that the emerging African is impatient with the speed with which desirable changes have come about. No fair-minded person, however, would stigmatize what has been achieved in the short history of this country as constituting 'oppression'. Indeed, these beneficent changes could not possibly have resulted from oppression. Beyond question the progress has been the result of co-operation between the races and, should it come to an end, progress will cease and there will be a sharp retrogression in every aspect of life for all the inhabitants of this country.

The charge of oppression levelled against the European of this country by the appellant is as a generalisation false and provides a spurious justification for the terrorist atrocities committed against the civilian population. If any generalisation is to be made it is that the progress made by Africans under European rule has been remarkable and much greater than the progress made over the same period of time in any other African country.

No country in the history of the world can claim to have established a system of government or institutions which at any given time have been perfect and Rhodesia is no exception to the general rule. What is certain is that nothing has happened in the very short and successful history of Rhodesia remotely to justify the bestial acts of terrorism committed against civilians and, what is no less certain is that on a balanced and comprehensive assessment of all that has been achieved, it is a monstrous travesty of the truth to describe the history of this country under European rule as one of oppression.

The only oppression in the recent history of Rhodesia occurred during the short period of the Matabele domination from 1840–1893, the year in which the Matabele were defeated by the Pioneers. That defeat ended the despotic reign of Lobengula, who had kept the whole of this country in thrall by the barbaric and savage use of witchcraft and the unbridled use of military power. For a detailed account of the excesses committed during this period and the life of the ordinary African before the conquest of Matabeleland, such works as the *Diaries of the Jesuit Missionaries at Bulawayo from 1879–1881* should be consulted. The diaries conclude with the following assessment of the Matabele at that time:

> Living entirely by pillage and by war, they seem to refuse any progress at all and are, in this respect, the most backward and the most barbarous of all the natives of Southern Africa.

That that stricture is not true today is a tribute to the co-operation between African and European, a co-operation which has outlawed internecine tribal war and pillage and which, to a very great extent, has eliminated the more barbaric practices of witchcraft.

Oppression by invaders of an indigenous people has, in a large number of countries, been characterised by the decimation of the indigenous inhabitants. It is quite unnecessary to mention the countries in which this has happened. They readily identify themselves and, paradoxically, are among Rhodesia's most strident critics. In Rhodesia the reverse has happened and with the establishment of law and order and the creation of a burgeoning economy, there has been a population explosion. A

116

fair-minded person will not readily accept that this could happen as a result of oppression.

Two main arguments were advanced by the appellant for not obeying the law. The first was that it would not be possible to keep open the various institutions under his jurisdiction if they were seen to be collaborating with the Government. The second was that the law that terrorists should be reported was unjust, that the terrorists are justified in taking up arms against the Government, because it is oppressive and that it would be wrong for 'any Christian worthy of the name' as well as any tribesman 'playing the traitor' to report them.

Subsidiary arguments are advanced in support of these two main arguments and, in addition, the appellant has raised a number of arguments unrelated to them.

The appellant also used the occasion to launch an attack on the Security Forces. This would seem to be part of his general attack on the Government. Conscious of the fact that it would be inexcusable to collaborate with the terrorists by refusing to report them if they were guilty of the atrocities against the African and European civilian population attributed to them and that it would be even more inexcusable for a Roman Catholic prelate to do so if the terrorists belonged to a Communist organisation, the appellant, in his statement, mentions that he has 'heard' and has been 'told' by the Government propaganda agencies and by the RBC and the RTV of these atrocities and the fact that they have been committed by Communist terrorists, but casts doubt on these sources by saying:

'I must say at once that personally I doubt every bit of Government propaganda that I hear on the RBC or RTV, just as I read with the greatest

sense of scepticism much that is printed in our
Rhodesian newspapers.'

In the result, the appellant manages to convey the
impression that, while the Security Forces are evil
and should not be supported, the terrorists are
justified in taking up arms.

But in marked contrast to his attitude to the
Security Forces, the appellant adroitly avoids ex-
pressing any view on whether or not the terrorists
are guilty of atrocities against the civilian population and whether or not they are Communist.
While claiming an unrivalled knowledge of what is
happening in the operational area and using this
knowledge as a basis for his attack on the Security
Forces, he omits to say what his own information
concerning the terrorists is or to say what this
information leads him to believe.

In common with all reasonably well-informed
persons living in this country the appellant knows
only too well what the terrorists are doing but, to
confess this and reveal the nature of their actions,
would reveal his stand for what it is; support for
Communist terrorists who do not shrink from
committing the most bestial acts against defenceless
civilians not in any way actively involved in the
struggle between the terrorists and the Security
Forces. The appellant, in company with the World
Council of Churches, adopts the tactic of condemn-
ing all acts of violence, but at the same time
studiously refrains from identifying the perpetrators
of the crimes involved whenever the evidence points
unerringly in the direction of the terrorists. By
refusing to identify the perpetrators of such acts
when they are committed by terrorists, the appellant
manages to convey the idea that since the acts must,
of necessity, have been committed by one side or the

other the Security Forces could possibly be responsible for them. His dishonest conduct in this regard is particularly reprehensible in a person occupying such a high clerical office.

In the result the appellant nowhere in his very long statement acknowledges that terrorists belong to a Marxist/Leninist organization. From the innumerable terrorist cases which have come before this Court as well as from other sources, the following facts are notorious:

1. Many terrorists have received their training in Russia, China and Eastern European countries under Russian domination.

2. Many who have not been trained in countries outside Africa have been trained by Communist instructors in Tanzania and other African countries orientated towards Communism.

3. In the result, the tactics used by the terrorists are similar to those used by Communists in subverting law and order in other parts of the world.

4. The terrorists operate from Mozambique which makes no secret of the fact that it has embraced Marxist/Leninist principles.

5. It is improbable that terrorists would be acceptable to the Mozambique Government if they embraced a wholly different political philosophy.

6. It is inconceivable that Mozambique would allow, much less welcome, the establishment of a system of government in this country different from and opposed to its own, and Mozambique is in the position of being able to dictate to the terrorists at the present time.

7. The terrorists' debt to their Communist sponsors is such that it would be unreasonable to

expect that in the unlikely event of their achieving victory they would forsake the Communists and transfer their allegiance to the countries of the Western World. In the light of the fact that Russia is steadily expanding its influence in Africa, while at the same time and to a corresponding extent the countries of the Western World withdraw, it is too much to expect that such a transfer of allegiance would come about.

8. Statements have been made by the terrorist leaders that a solution to the problems of Rhodesia can only be brought about by violence. The idea that revolutionary change can only be brought about by violence is a corner stone of the Communist philosophy and is expressed in the following words by Marx in his Communist manifesto:

> The Communists disdain to conceal their views and aims. They openly declare that their ends can be attained only by the forcible overthrow of all existing social conditions.

9. Before a Special Court convened to consider the detention of the Rev Ndabaningi Sithole, documentary evidence was led by the State to establish that the terrorists were a Communist organisation. The documents consisted of the official pamphlets published by the terrorist organisation and their authenticity was not challenged by Mr Maisels, Q.C., who appeared for the Rev Ndabaningi Sithole. The documents were obviously authentic and were available for inspection by the press and members of the public. They showed beyond any doubt at all that the terrorist organisation

operating from Mozambique has adopted the Marxist/Leninist principles. A copy of the judgement is annexed to this judgement.

Communism is not only atheistic, it is actively anti-Christian and since the appellant acknowledges to quote his own words that 'The whole reason for my office is that I should dedicate myself completely to the work of advancing the Christian Religion', he must necessarily take up the position that in collaborating with the terrorists by refusing to report their presence to the Security Forces, he is not collaborating with a Communist organisation. He attempts to establish, as far as it is in his limited power to do so, that the terrorists are a respectable organisation, fighting with every justification against an oppressive government. That this is the image he seeks to create for them is shown very clearly by the following passages in his statement dealing with the terrorists:

'I had heard too that this ideology (the appellant is referring to the Marxist ideology) was shared by those who came armed into Rhodesia determined to achieve equality under the law and equal opportunity for all the citizens of Rhodesia. It seemed vitally important to me that these people should not, on their contact with the Church in Rhodesia, be made to believe that it collaborated with the régime which they considered oppressive. Rather it was necessary for the Church, as represented by our Missions, to manifest a courageous and generous Christian concern, even for the wayward.

This was the first thing which decided my thinking in regard to the attitude to be adopted by the missionaries should they be approached by terrorists.

And the appellant poses the question:

'Is the missionary-informer not responsible for the death of any young man or woman who, in defence of his own fundamental rights, takes up arms for what he believes is a just cause?'

It will be noticed that the appellant, in the first passage cited above, uses the words 'I had heard too' and not 'I knew that this Marxist ideology was shared' by them. Had the appellant confessed he knew they were Marxist/Leninist terrorists, could he then have said, as he did, that they 'came armed into Rhodesia, determined to achieve equality under the law and equal opportunity for all the citizens of Rhodesia'. Could this possibly be the appellant's assessment of what Communists do?

The appellant speaks of propaganda but is there a more subtle propaganda device than to state a fact as being no more than a rumour and to then offset the rumour by stating categorically that the terrorists are dedicated to 'achieving equality under the law and equal opportunity for all the citizens of Rhodesia'?

Dealing with the visit of terrorists to the Avila Mission on the night of 25th April, the appellant gives the following account of his conversation with Father X after the latter had left the Mission, and his reaction to Father X's departure from the mission:

'When I arrived there I heard *to my great dismay* That Father X had left the mission early in the morning, bringing with him the two Sisters and all their belongings because of threats from terrorists who had come to Avila the night before.

The story, as I heard it from him, was that on the previous night, while at supper, he and Sister Vianney were summoned out into the darkness by two men who had guns at the ready. When they met they saw some other armed men lurking in the shadows some distance away. *According to the priest,* he and the sister were lectured on the glories of Communism and the evils of capitalism as represented by the Kennedys, the Rockefellers and the Catholic Church. The visitors ordered the priest to reduce the school fees and the charges made at the Mission clinic. He replied that the clinic was unaided, receiving no support from the State, and that the sisters were unpaid and the medicines had to be bought by the Mission. The terrorists told him that the Church could well afford to provide medicines freely. They then threatened that the Mission would be destroyed and other vengeance taken if their other requests for watches, radios, cameras, etc., were not granted.

After a long interview, the men went off, the priest having told them that he could not possibly meet their demands.

Naturally both he and the other members of the Mission staff were greatly frightened by the visit, and they decided that it would be unsafe for them to remain there any longer. They packed up and left early next morning, drove to Inyanga, informed the civil authorities, and without further delay arrived at Triashill Mission, a hundred miles away from Avila, where I met them and heard their story.

The priest was very distraught and wondered if he had acted correctly in leaving the Mission and informing the authorities. I consoled him by saying that *if what he told me were true,* and that his night visitors were Communists who had said that they wanted to destroy the Church and its Missions, *then* he had acted correctly.' (My italics.)

In the course of this conversation, the appellant received from Father X the most cogent evidence that terrorists are in fact Communists and if he doubted Father X's uncorroborated evidence, it was always possible for him to obtain Sister Vianney's version of what was said and done by the terrorists. Notwithstanding the overwhelming evidence available to him on this occasion, it is of the greatest significance that the appellant uses the words in italics in the above passage. These words are intended to convey that until the appellant has heard the terrorists' version of what was said and done by them, he is not prepared to accept the version received from his own priest as being the truth. He says: *'The story, as I heard it from him, ...'* and *'... if what he told me were true, ... then* he acted correctly.' It could reasonably be expected that, having regard to the trust which should necessarily exist between a bishop and one of his priests, he would have said: "I consoled him by saying that since his night visitors were Communists who had said they wanted to destroy the Church and its Missions, he had acted correctly."

In the light of overwhelming evidence that the terrorists are Communists, it is amazing that the appellant, with his means of knowledge, should evade this fact; it is even more astounding that he should be at pains to avoid making a frank acknowledgement that the *modus operandi* of the terrorists is to attack African and European civilians, murdering and mutilating them, and to avoid contact with the Security Forces by every possible means, including threats that any person reporting their presence will be murdered. So notorious are the atrocities committed by the terrorists that knowledge of what they have done and are doing is shared by everyone living in this country and is certainly not confined to persons with access to the records of cases coming before the courts. The terrorists are selective in the atrocities they commit against African civilians – murder and mutilation is reserved for those Africans who oppose or are suspected of opposing them that is the so-called 'sell-outs'. European civilians, both male and female, with the exception of the Europeans working in the institutions under the appellant's jurisdiction, are murdered indiscriminately whenever the opportunity occurs. We deal elsewhere in this judgement with the reasons why the exception is made in the case of Europeans working under the appellant's jurisdiction.

The first of the appellant's main arguments, that it would not be possible to keep the various institutions under his jurisdiction open if the terrorists had reason to believe the personnel of these institutions were hostile to them and were reporting their presence to the Security Forces, is an argument of substance, and a strong mitigating factor. The recent massacre at Musami has shown conclusively that the terrorists do not stop short of murdering Roman Catholic missionaries.

It is understandable that the appellant is most reluctant to see institutions under his jurisdiction close down. Once personnel were dispersed, it would be extremely difficult, and might even prove impossible in some instances, to re-open. The appellant has devoted thirty years of his life to building up these institutions and their closure would be a bitter blow to him. The fact that the appellant has expressed views which are quite untenable and intemperate and that in some respects he has been dishonest, must not be allowed to obscure the dilemma in which the appellant is unquestionably placed by the situation which has developed.

It is necessary in assessing the strength of this mitigating factor to bear in mind that missionaries are not prepared, because of their religious convictions, to take up arms in defence of either the missions or their own lives. It follows that the various institutions are defenceless and it is acknowledged that it would not be possible for the Security Forces to provide every missionary institution in the operational area with a permanent guard. The only way in the circumstances in which the appellant, to use his own words, can 'guarantee the safety of his Sisters' and other personnel is to satisfy the terrorists that these institutions are well disposed towards them and, conversely, are hostile to the Government and that they can be relied upon not to report their presence in the area. The appellant, we are satisfied, has succeeded in convincing the terrorists of this and it is for that reason that no institution under his control has been attacked, notwithstanding that they are all in the operational area and that some are very close to the border. While this reason for the appellant's desire to collaborate with the terrorists, by not reporting their presence, clearly emerges, it is not a reason which this Court accepts as valid and, for the reasons given elsewhere in this judgement, it cannot possibly serve the long-term interests of the Roman Catholic Church. Nevertheless, in assessing the appropriate sentence, full weight must be given to it. The appellant also says:

'I told my missionaries that I would hold myself entirely responsible for their actions, both in giving medicines to the terrorists and in not reporting their presence. In doing so, I am convinced, not only that I was acting correctly as their Bishop, but that I was actually fulfilling a further obligation, namely of taking more care of the defenceless missionaries than of the armed forces, who, I presumed, were well able and well equipped to defend themselves. In short, I believe my greater duty, from every point of view, lay in protecting the lives of innocent and defenceless people than in protecting soldiers'.

This reason, if it stood alone, would be a very strong mitigating factor, because, for the reasons which I have given earlier in this judgement, there is no doubt at all that missionaries are placed in a most invidious position. It is very clear, however, that the appellant has been motivated to a large extent by sympathy for the terrorists and hostility towards the Government. He says, for example:

'In fact in many cases the Security Forces are already aware that terrorists are around. They obtain this information as a result of their own activities, and they also get it from the hundreds of paid informers, *people who are prepared to play the traitor*, very often simply to revenge themselves on their own personal enemies.'

The words 'prepared to play the traitor' reveal the extent of the appellant's sympathy for the terrorists. They reveal that the appellant believes that members of the public, who are not in the invidious position of a minister of religion, should also refuse to report. The view is clearly expressed that no person, Christian or pagan, should assist the Government by reporting terrorists. Tribesmen also face difficulties and problems in reporting as this Court has had occasion to point out in a series of judgements, but these difficulties are of an entirely different kind and the view contained in the above statement shows the extravagant lengths to which the appellant is prepared to go in justifying his attitude.

The appellant makes a point that it is not always

possible for a person to serve both God and the State and that an informed Christian conscience not infrequently dictates that a person 'please God, not men'. What the appellant has done in the commission of these offences is undoubtedly extremely displeasing to many men in Rhodesia. On the other hand, his conduct must necessarily be extremely pleasing to the men who make up the terrorist gangs, and such as to endear him to them. This is necessarily so since it is an attitude which ensures that, so long as the appellant is in charge, neither he nor anyone acting on his advice will report the presence of terrorists in his diocese. This means that terrorists may come and go from any of the institutions under his control without fear of a report being made to the Security Forces by any member of the institution. This must be well known to the terrorists by now since express directions have been given by the appellant to all persons under his jurisdiction not to report and, as the appellant rightly says, there is the closest contact between the various institutions and the African people of the areas which they cover. In his address he indicates clearly that the safety of the staff and the various institutions under his control is dependent on the terrorists being made fully aware that these institutions are not 'collaborating' with the men who constitute the Government.

The appellant devotes much of his statement to showing how it comes about there is a coincidence between his belief that what he has done and is doing is pleasing to God and the fact that his actions must unquestionably be pleasing and a continuing source of comfort to the men who make up the terrorist gangs in his area. To show that this coincidence in no way invalidates his belief that what he is doing 'pleases God', the appellant sets out to make a case that the real villains are not the men who constitute the terrorist gangs, but the Europeans, in particular the Europeans who constitute the Government, and the members of the Security Forces of all races. In his enthusiasm to establish this premise he falls into the understandable but inexcusable error in a man of such erudition and in such a calling, of grossly exaggerating the faults of the men he condemns and grossly understating the faults of those with whom he collaborates. The appellant, in the course of his statement said:

> 'Were we and all other Christian missionaries to be forced to close down all these institutions by being compelled to violate conscience and obey the laws of men rather than those of God, Rhodesia would very greatly suffer.'

The reason for closing down would, in fact, as the appellant admits elsewhere in his statement, result directly from the hostility of the Communist terrorists and only indirectly from compliance by the institutions under the appellant's jurisdiction with the law that persons should report a terrorist presence. But the appellant, in the above passage, by a process of circuitous reasoning, attempts to establish that the blame for any such closure would be attributable not to the activities of the Communist terrorists but to compulsion brought to bear on those institutions by the Government 'to violate conscience and obey the laws of men rather than those of God . . .' In short, collaboration with the terrorists and refusal to collaborate with Government, by this process of circuitous reasoning, becomes 'the divine law through the mediation of conscience, properly informed'. By collaborating with the Communist terrorists, the appellant, in the result, sees himself as 'obeying God and not men'. It is only possible to comment that the appellant is possessed of a singularly malleable conscience, capable of being shaped in a most unusual way to accord with his preconceived ideas. The appellant continues:

'One may well ask, is this what the Government wants? Is this what the legislation we are dealing with envisages? I might well ask myself also which is better, to keep my missions in existence and my missionaries in the field for the general good of Rhodesia, a good which can be equated with the good of the Christian church, or must I, in blind obedience, obey a particular ordinance of men and so bring the whole work of Christianity to an end?'

This statement postulates that the good of the Church is to be measured in the short term, that if the missions and other institutions are forced to close down, the whole work of Christianity is brought to an end. The truth, as we see it, is that what would bring 'the whole work of Christianity to an end' permanently is not the temporary closure of any of the appellant's institutions made necessary by the need to fight and overcome Communist terrorism, but the victory of Communism in this country. It is not understood how a person with the appellant's background and high office in the Roman Catholic Church can overlook the long-term interests of Christianity and adopt the short-term expediency of collaboration with Communist terrorism, a collaboration which, if it led to a Communist victory, could only spell the end of everything the appellant maintains he stands for. There would not, with a Communist victory, be "a continuing presence of the Christian Church and a consequent benefit to Rhodesia now and in the years to come'', as the appellant says in his statement. It is charitable to believe that the appellant is not being deliberately dishonest when he implies very clearly that collaboration with the terrorists and opposition to the present Government is 'the imperative of the divine law through the mediation of conscience, properly informed', but rather that his hostility to the Government has become obsessive and has led to a situation in which he has become blinded by his bias to any other point of view.

The appellant's high regard for the Communist terrorists and his corresponding contempt for the Security Forces fighting against them is manifest in the following passages:

'Closely connected with this argument is the fact that the Security Forces are not really in control of the situation anywhere in the operational area of Rhodesia. I say this in spite of all the State propaganda to the contrary.'

'All the Security Forces are able to do is to move into an area where terrorists are reported to have appeared, carry out punitive raids, stay on for a little while and then move on to another disturbed area to do the same.

Moreover, the strength of the African people's opposition to the present Government is daily on the increase. Time and numbers are on their side, and they know it. No matter what the State propaganda may declare, the African people already sense that the Security Forces are no longer in control of events.

The practice of informing is, as far as the successful prosecution of the war goes, quite useless. The Security Forces generally only manage to kill innocent villagers in retaliation for the presence of guerrillas. Moreover, by such action they not only further antagonise the African people, but they promote the cause of those whom they seek to eliminate.'

The above passages from the appellant's statement are all part of the appellant's theme that the terrorists are going to win and there is a note of exultation in the passages. Had a Communist propagandist set out to give comfort and encouragement to the terrorists, it would not have been possible for him to have done better than the appellant has in these passages. His words reveal not the balanced and moderate viewpoint of a prelate, but the diatribe of a political activist, anxious to promote by any means the victory of Communist terrorism. The appellant dare not admit that the terrorists are both bestial and Communist and dare not even admit that this is a possibility because once he does, the whole of his violent and intemperate opposition to the Security Forces and his collaboration on the other hand with the terrorists, would become suspect to say the least. In his statement the appellant says:

'I am not an anarchist' and at another point:

'I believe that I was not acting as an anarchist', and also

'In all my criticism there was nothing whatsoever of a spirit of anarchy.'

Why should it be necessary for a bishop to emphasise more than once in the course of his statement that he is not an anarchist? In the ordinary way, his calling and position would be sufficient to make such a suggestion absurd. The appellant is, however, aware that collaboration with the terrorists and opposition to the Government of the kind evinced in his statement, is conduct which is calculated to encourage persons who respect his opinion as a prelate to indulge in revolutionary action. It is no use for a bishop who employs inflammatory language to protest that he is against violence. If he is truly against violence, let him refrain from using language which leads logically and inevitably to it. A young African, with little knowledge of the achievements which have been brought about by the very successful co-operation between the races in Rhodesia over a very short period of time and of the changes which have steadily taken place, would, on hearing the words of the appellant laying stress in extravagant language on the allegedly evil and oppressive conduct of the European and Government, be left in no doubt that he should resort to violence in order to overthrow the Government.

The appellant in his statement raises a number of excuses for his conduct unrelated to his two main arguments mentioned earlier in this judgement. He says:

'The Christian clergyman, in terms of his very function, must appear to men as offering to them the mercy and reconciliation of his God. No one, even the greatest criminal, the most debased, the most hardened sinner, may ever be refused his counsel or his words of mercy.'

This is another excuse which simply does not bear examination. The terrorists did not on any of the occasions on which the appellant failed to report, come to him for 'his counsel or his words of mercy'. Since they are fighting in a Communist organisation, it is most improbable that they are practising Christians. He says:

'But there is another possible variation in the case. Suppose, for instance, I am conducting a

133

religious service, and I notice, or have brought to my attention by others, an enemy of the State amongst the congregation of worshippers. Am I supposed to report his presence to the Security Forces, and so make his act of worship the occasion of capture or death? Is obedience to the State to be regarded as the greater good to be sought and obtained than an individual's act of acknowledging the worship he owes to his God? Am I, the minister of religion, to play the turncoat and become the servant of the State rather than the servant of God? In other words, am I bound to obey men rather than God?'

Once again, these were not the circumstances in which the appellant failed to report the presence of terrorists. Had they been, it is quite possible the Attorney-General would not have instituted a prosecution. He says:

'The danger of reporting terrorists who deliberately make their presence known is that the terrorists might be laying a trap for the Security Forces. If this succeeds, the African missionary may be accused of being a party to the trap.'

Any excuse, no matter how far-fetched, is used in justification of his failure to obey the law. When such an improbable argument as that above is used, the inference to be drawn is that there is an absence of sincerity in advancing it.

In justification of his conduct the appellant cites a number of directives received from the Holy See of his Church. We have read these directives and we are satisfied that they do not direct priests to become involved in political activity and cannot be reasonably interpreted as doing so. In particular we are satisfied that these directives do not direct that priests should become actively engaged in dismantl-

134

ing political structures or systems. To attack the structure or system of a government would bring the Church and State into conflict. Such a conflict would only be justified where the State, as in Communist countries, attempts to suppress the Church itself. It is unlikely, we think, that it can be the policy of the Roman Catholic Church to permit a priest to indulge in political activities of the kind mentioned by the appellant in his statement. Nor are we impressed by the attempt he makes to elevate purely secular and political issues to the spiritual plane. Political activity by a priest can only lead to dissension and controversy within the Church he serves and the appellant's revelation in his statement that an official request was made to Pope Paul by some members of the laity of his Church to remove him from his office comes as no surprise.

While we agree that the factors which the trial court took into account in arriving at sentence were properly taken into account, we are of the opinion that insufficient weight was given to the dilemma which missionaries experience in their struggle and determination to keep their missions and other institutions open in the operational areas. In a series of judgements this Court has emphasised that persons who are in an invidious position when the duty arises of making a report are not to be punished as severely as those who are not. We are satisfied that because of the failure of the trial court to give sufficient weight to this aspect of the case the sentence imposed was manifestly excessive.

As stated earlier in this judgement the safety of missionaries in the operational areas depends, regrettably, to a large extent on their ability to satisfy the terrorist organisation that they are not hostile to it. It is very clear indeed that the terrorists

135

because they are Communists, have no respect at all for the sanctity of a Church or of the priests and nuns who serve it.

But for the seriously aggravating factors in the appellant's conduct referred to in this judgement, the dilemma which exists and the invidious position of the priests and nuns in the light of that dilemma would make a substantial prison sentence inappropriate. Because of those aggravating factors, however, a substantial prison sentence is called for.

Having studied the appellant's statement with care we are conscious of the fact that the appellant believes that any sentence imposed on him will be unjust and that by going to prison he will suffer martyrdom.

In his statement, the appellant deals with the subject of martyrdom. Referring to the views of the Superior under whom he studied in Rome, he says:

'Over and over again he warned us that the age of martyrdom would never leave the Church and that some of us might even be called to enjoy that privilege',

and he ends his statement by quoting the words of St. Peter:

'No one can hurt you if you are determined to do only what is right. If you do have to suffer for being good, you will count it a blessing. There is no need to be afraid or to worry about them. Simply reverence the Lord Christ in your hearts, and always have your answer ready for people who ask you the reason for the hope that you all have. But give it with courtesy and respect and with a clear conscience, so that those who slander you when you are living a good life in Christ may be proved wrong in the accusations that they bring. And if it is the will of God that you should suffer, it is better to suffer for doing right than for doing wrong.'

The appellant, unhappily, appears to be under the impression that his judgement of what is right or wrong is infallible, and that those who challenge his judgement are wrong, even 'moral primitives', and that should he be punished it will be given to him 'to enjoy the privilege' of martyrdom and the satisfaction of suffering 'for doing what is right' rather 'than for doing what is wrong'. We entertain no doubt that the appellant would enjoy the notoriety of serving a prison sentence.

From the purely subjective point of view, therefore, a prison sentence will serve no purpose but such a sentence is necessary to mark the seriousness of the offence and to deter others from behaving in the same way.

In substitution of the sentence imposed by the trial court and giving full weight to the submissions of counsel, we would impose the following sentence:

Four years' imprisonment with labour, three years of which will be suspended for five years on condition that the appellant is not convicted during that period of any offence under the Law and Order (Maintenance) Act [Cap. 65] and sentenced to imprisonment without the option of a fine.

II. AN INDEPENDENT REPORT

The report on Bishop Lamont's trial which follows is by Seamus Henchy, Judge of the Supreme Court of Ireland, who attended the trial on behalf of the International Commission of Jurists.

Appearances

The accused was represented by Mr Lionel Weinstock, S.C., of the South African Bar, Mr A. Gubbay, S.C., of the Rhodesian Bar, and Mr C. Jordan (instructed by Mr M. Muller of Messrs Scanlen and Holderness).

Mr J. A. R. Giles and Mr I. Donovan appeared for the prosecution.

The Court

The court of trial was the court of a regional magistrate, Mr W. R. Henning, who sat with two assessors.

The offences charged carried a sentence of death or life imprisonment under s. 51(1)(c) of the Law and Order (Maintenance) Act, 1970, but, because the trial was before a regional magistrate, his sentencing powers were limited by s. 63(1)(c) of that Act to a fine not exceeding 2,000 Rhodesian dollars or imprisonment for a period not exceeding fifteen years.

The Plea

Before the accused pleaded to the charges, his

counsel submitted that Counts 1 and 2 amounted to an impermissible splitting of a single offence. He submitted that Count 1 should be quashed on the ground that it was simply the completed offence charged in Count 2 with the added ingredient of incitement, and that on the authorities an accused could be charged with inciting another to commit an offence which he had jointly committed with that other.

Having heard legal argument, the magistrate refused the application to quash Count 1.

The accused then pleaded guilty to all four Counts.

The Facts

The essential facts in relation to the four Counts were agreed to be those set out in a written statement of agreed facts handed in to the Court with the consent of counsel for the prosecution and of counsel for the defence.

The Evidence

The only evidence called by the prosecution was that of Detective Officer Williams of the Rhodesian Special Branch, who dealt mainly with geographical and locational matters, including the nature and disposition of Security Forces in the relevant area at the time of the charges.

The only witnesses called for the defence were the Anglican Bishop of Mashonaland (which includes Salisbury), Rt Rev Paul Burrough, and the Anglican Bishop of Matabeleland, Rt Rev Mark Wood. Both of those witnesses gave their evidence after the accused had made his address to the Court, but without having heard that address. Their evidence stressed the dilemma of Church authorities

when mission workers are visited by terrorists. They
both said they found it impossible to give a 'straight
reply' as to what they would do in the accused's
position when a mission had been visited by
terrorists seeking medical supplies. Bishop Burrough said that if the terrorists did not threaten
violence he would not report them; otherwise he
would. He would not give a general direction to
mission personnel not to report terrorists who came
to them. Both bishops expressed the view that
whether they would instruct or incite mission
personnel not to report the presence of terrorists
would depend on the circumstances of the particular
case; it was a moral decision to be made in each case
in the light of the particular circumstances of the
case.

The accused's address to the Court

Bishop Lamont stated that he would not give
sworn testimony, for the sole reason that by doing so
he would leave himself open to cross-examination
which would elicit from him answers which might
incriminate particular priests and nuns in his
diocese. Instead, he elected to give an unsworn
statement from the dock. This unsworn statement
was made from a lengthy written document in five
parts, each part of which was handed in to the Court
in turn. Some alterations and interpolations were
made in the written version as it was being delivered.

Counsel's closing address

Mr Weinstock, in addressing the Court on behalf
of the accused, was naturally circumscribed, not
only by the plea of guilty, but also by the manner in
which the accused in his unsworn statement had
justified his conduct. He urged that the accused was

not a man of violence who had opted for the course of assisting terrorists. Rather, he was a man who opposed violence and who, when confronted with the dilemma of deciding whether Sister Vianney or he should report the presence of terrorists in the Inyanga mission, made a conscientious decision not to report, in the interests of the safety of those working in the mission. He suggested to the magistrate that, in exercise of the powers vested in him by s. 337 of the Criminal Procedure and Evidence Act, 1970, he should suspend the operation of any sentence imposed or, alternatively, postpone the passing of sentence for a period not less than the three years allowed by that section, subject to such conditions as he might think proper to impose.

On the 23rd September 1976 the magistrate postponed his judgement on sentence until the 1st October 1976.

The Sentence

On the 1st October 1976 the magistrate imposed a sentence ten years' imprisonment with hard labour. By then I had left Rhodesia, so I did not hear the reasons put forward by the magistrate for the measurement of punishment in those terms. A transcript of the judgement has not yet come to hand. I understand, however, that the sentence imposed was stated to be deterrent as well as punitive, and was so imposed on the ground that the accused had misused his position of authority by giving, and inciting the giving of, aid to terrorists, because he had not expressed any regret for doing so, and because in his statement in court he had attacked the Government of Rhodesia and not the terrorists. Apparently, the only matters reckoned in his favour were his age and the fact that he had pleaded guilty.

Observations

The trial, as I saw it, was conducted in a fair and courteous manner. Criticism, if it is to be made, must be directed against the nature of the offences charged and against the severity of the sentence.

The dilemma in which Bishop Lamont found himself is but another addition to the tragic catalogue of cases of persons caught up in the struggle between the Rhodesian Security Forces and the terrorists. The evils resulting from the measures adopted by the Rhodesian authorities for dealing with that armed conflict have been highlighted in the ICJ Report on *Racial Discrimination and Repression in Southern Rhodesia*. The law bears so harshly and arbitrarily on a person who unwillingly finds himself assisting terrorists that any missionary or other person in one of the 'operational areas' of Rhodesia might easily be charged, convicted and sentenced as Bishop Lamont has been.

It would, of course, be tragic if Bishop Lamont, who is now sixty-six years old and who has given the past thirty years of his life in the service of the people of Umtali, black and white equally, were to become one of the first prisoners of conscience in the new state of Zimbabwe which is about to replace Rhodesia. At present he is on bail pending appeal, and it seems likely that his appeal will not be heard until well into 1977. By then the legal background of the case may be overshadowed by political developments, for those now labelled terrorists or supporters of terrorists may have come to share political power. It is to be hoped that a political settlement will carry with it an amnesty for those imprisoned under the present emergency legislation. Even if there is no general amnesty, there is a strong case to be made for giving special consideration to Bishop Lamont's case. If his sentence is allowed to stand, the missionary work of the Christian churches, which is so important in Rhodesia, will be imperilled, for all missionaries in the 'operational areas' will be at risk. More particularly, the life-work of a great humanitarian will have been cruelly and prematurely cut short. It is to be hoped that the International Commission of Jurists will use its good offices to ensure that those charged with bringing the state of Zimbabwe into existence will undo the sentence on Bishop Lamont – if it has not already been set aside on appeal. His statement to the court that tried him proclaims him to be a man of principle, courage, compassion and talent. It would be wholly regrettable if his life's contribution to the people of Rhodesia, in particular the black people of Rhodesia, were to be snuffed out by his harsh sentence.